THE WADSWORTH ENGLISH FOR ACADEMIC PURPOSES SERIES

Series Editors:
Charles H. Blatchford, Fair Oaks, California
Jerry L. Messec, Florida State University

Academically Speaking
Janet Kayfetz, University of California, Santa Barbara
Randy Stice, Nova University, Florida

Academic Writing Workshop
Sarah Benesch, College of Staten Island, CUNY
Mia Rakijas, New York City, New York
Betsy Rorschach, City College, CUNY

Academic Writing Workshop II
Sarah Benesch, College of Staten Island, CUNY
Betsy Rorschach, City College, CUNY

English on Campus: A Listening Sampler
Sharon Bode, Bradenton, Florida
Charles G. Whitley, Chaminade University
Gary James, Honolulu Community College

Overheard and Understood
Sharon Bode, Bradenton, Florida
Sandra Moulding Lee, Linfield College

Improving the Grammar of Written English: The Handbook
Patricia Byrd, Georgia State University
Beverly Benson, DeKalb College

Improving the Grammar of Written English: The Editing Process
Beverly Benson, DeKalb College
Patricia Byrd, Georgia State University

Understanding Conversations
Catherine Tansey, Tokyo, Japan
Charles H. Blatchford, Fair Oaks, California

Academic Writing Workshop II

Sarah Benesch
College of Staten Island, CUNY

Betsy Rorschach
City College, CUNY

Wadsworth Publishing Company
Belmont, California
A Division of Wadsworth, Inc.

Series Editors: Charles H. Blatchford and Jerry L. Messec
English/ESL Editor: Angela Gantner
Production Editor: Vicki Friedberg
Cover and Interior Designer: Andrew H. Ogus
Print Buyer: Randy Hurst
Permissions Editor: Robert M. Kauser
Copy Editor: Melissa Andrews
Compositor: Graphic Typesetting Service
Cover Collage: Bill Reuter

Printed in the United States of America   49

1 2 3 4 5 6 7 8 9 10—93 92 91 90 89

Library of Congress Cataloging-in-Publication Data

Benesch, Sarah.
    Academic writing workshop II / Sarah Benesch, Betsy Rorschach.
      p.   cm. — (The Wadsworth English for academic purposes
series)
    Includes index.
    ISBN 0-534-07561-4
    1. English language—Textbooks for foreign speakers.   2. English
language—Rhetoric.   I. Rorschach, Betsy.   II. Title.   III. Title:
Academic writing workshop two.   IV. Title: Academic writing workshop
2.   V. Series.
PE1128.B4464 1989
    808'.042—dc19   88-18093
                                                                CIP

Contents

Chapter 2/Writing About What You Are Learning   20

Chapter 3/Revising and Editing What You Have Written   35

UNIT TWO/ WRITING ABOUT SOCIAL SCIENCES   49

Chapter 4/Culture Shock   50

Chapter 5/Language and Society   62

Chapter 6/Children's Lives   73

UNIT THREE/
WRITING ABOUT APPLIED SCIENCES   85

Chapter 7/The Role of a Scientist   86

Chapter 8/Chemistry   100

Chapter 9/Engineering and Computer Technology   111

UNIT FOUR/ WRITING ABOUT HUMANITIES   125

Chapter 10/Visual Arts   126

Chapter 11/Poetry   137

Chapter 12/Publishing   149

Appendix/Supplementary Readings   158

About the Wadsworth EAP Series

The Wadsworth English for Academic Purposes (EAP) series provides appropriate learning materials for university courses that focus on the academic uses of English. The EAP series has been planned to help ESL students communicate competently in all aspects of academic life in the United States. The materials support learning of academic-level skills in reading, writing, listening, and speaking. They can be used in intensive or nonintensive formats, in classroom, group, or individual study, and for courses of varying lengths.

The Wadsworth EAP series is based on three principles:

1. **Comprehensive Skills Development:** The series views language skills as integrated, so each book not only stands on its own but also builds on and relates to other texts in the series. Books targeted for all skill areas maintain a consistent yet nonrepetitive approach.

2. **Academic Community Context:** The series provides practice in the varied language uses that students will encounter in their academic careers. Teaching and learning activities are in the context of college or university classroom or campus life. This context-specific approach respects the learning skills and educational background of students at academic English centers.

3. **Student-Centered, Process-Oriented Materials:** The series places student learning activities at the heart of each lesson and requires

students to take responsibility for their active role in the learning process.

The components of the Wadsworth EAP series include:

—**A grammar reference guide and handbook** that encourages students to identify specific grammar problems and practice language appropriate to specific academic contexts.

—**Listening comprehension texts and tapes** that develop listening skills to the high level necessary for achievement in an academic program.

—**Reading skill development books** that provide opportunity to practice the skills needed to read authentic academic texts with purpose and understanding.

—**Progressive process-oriented writing texts** that develop academic writing skills from brief reports to rigorous research tasks.

—**Spoken language texts** that provide progressive communicative practice to the level demanded of international students in academic programs.

The authors of the Wadsworth EAP series are experienced teachers in academic programs and have developed their materials from their classroom experience. However, the series is not "teacher-proof." The books do not attempt to provide all the "correct" answers, nor do they set down a strict step-by-step approach. The ambiguity of language at this level and the importance of developing interpretative skills are emphasized by the authors.

Although no one book is ideal for all students (or for all teachers), these books will stimulate and encourage everyone who is willing to participate fully in student-centered classes. The authors have written books that they hope will broaden students' vision and empower them with the expanding possibilities of language.

Control and support must come not only from the books themselves but also from the teachers who work with students and from the students themselves who strive to become responsible for their learning. Just as students seek to make the language serve their needs, so teachers need to use materials to support their individual pedagogical styles and approaches to language-learning problems.

In sum, the Wadsworth EAP series seeks to do more than prepare students for an examination in language skills. It seeks to help international students master academic English in order to achieve their academic goals. The authors of these texts have shared their experiences in providing opportunities for students to fulfill their academic potential—and isn't that what each of us would like to achieve?

Charles H. Blatchford and Jerry L. Messec
Series Editors

Preface

When the two of us decided to write this book, we had several goals in mind. First of all, we wanted to use what we knew about how people learn to write and improve as writers. We believe strongly that focusing on the process of writing leads to improvement, and we wanted to incorporate process approaches into our book.

Second, we feel strongly that ESL students need to work within academic areas as they acquire competence in the language. So frequently, ESL courses have no academic content; that is, the students are reading and writing but usually about various nonacademic topics that bear little or no relation to what they are studying or hope to study in their other courses. Consequently, they have trouble transferring what they learn about reading and writing in their ESL classes to the work they must do for their other courses.

We also wanted to set up situations in which the students would be active learners—situations that involve collaboration with a partner, in a small group, or with the entire class. The students are asked to collaborate as they read, take notes, plan their writing, revise, and edit. The collaboration not only leads to a better understanding of the material that the students are working on but also creates a language-rich classroom environment where speaking, listening, reading, and writing are connected.

To meet these goals, we designed a book that draws on theory about language acquisition, developmental writing abilities, and the role of writing in the learning process.

Fluency, Clarity, Correctness

The greatest obstacle we face in our ESL writing classes is our students' fear of making mistakes. Although we accept the fact that mistakes are part of the learning process, our students often avoid the embarrassment of making mistakes in both their writing and speaking. They write very little in order to minimize their errors. It is therefore essential to invite students to keep the flow of their ideas going as they write, without attending to mistakes. Fluency is encouraged through the use of the Academic Journal and through the frequent assignment of short, informal drafts. Clarity, the ability to make connections between ideas and communicate them to an audience, is encouraged through attention to revision. After taking notes and writing drafts, the students are asked to share their writing, get feedback, and revise. It is only after these drafts are revised and shared with the teacher that the students are asked to edit. The purpose of correcting is to create a piece that could be published in the class magazine, which the students put together in the last chapter.

Writing as a Tool for Learning

We often hear students complain that ESL courses are unrelated to the academic courses they plan to take. They feel frustrated when asked to complete assignments that have no connection to their academic interests. Yet, they also realize that they need some type of preparation to enter the mainstream, where they are asked to listen to lectures, take notes, read difficult texts, and participate in class discussions. *Academic Writing Workshop II* bridges the gap between language and academic content courses by providing assignments that ask students to read, discuss, and respond in writing to texts in the social sciences, applied sciences, and humanities. The note-taking techniques (dialogue notes and double-entry notes) are included to help students participate more actively in their own reading. By asking students to share their notes and then write essays based on the notes and follow-up discussions, we are showing them how to connect reading and writing to deepen their understanding of what they are learning.

The Interactive ESL Classroom

Our students are often surprised at the degree of participation called for in American college classes. Students are expected to ask questions and to consult the professor or one another if they are confused. Peer group work is one way to encourage greater participation on the part of each student. It forces the kind of responsibility that is missing when the whole class meets, with the teacher standing in front of the class. This is not to say that we have eliminated the whole-class setting, but we do provide frequent opportunities for the students to meet in pairs and small groups. In these settings, everyone talks and shares what he or she has written in preparation for the meeting. Peer groups allow for the formation of a community of writers, working collaboratively to improve as writers and as users of English.

Acknowledgments

Writing this book involved collaboration on many levels, and we would like to thank the various people who helped us throughout the process. Our students at City College and at the College of Staten Island wrote the sample texts that we have used here, making it possible for us to include examples for other students to read and study. Our reviewers, Gilbert D. Couts, The American University; Eva Dickson, North Texas State University; Lynn Henrichsen, Brigham Young University at Hawaii; Sarah J. Klinghammer, University of Oregon; Lois Kleinhenn Lanier, University of Maryland; Ron Schofield, University of California at Riverside; and Elizabeth Templin, University of Arizona; gave us useful feedback that helped us resee and revise the book. Most of all, Steve Rutter, Vicki Friedberg, and Andrew Ogus—the Wadsworth editorial staff—and Charley Blatchford and Jerry Messec, the series editors, gave us the support and encouragement we needed to finish what we had begun.

Introduction
to Teachers

Academic Writing Workshop II is an intermediate-level text that will help ESL students write for college courses. The assignments give students practice in using writing as a tool for learning and for understanding better what they are reading. The book elicits informal academic writing, such as journal entries, note taking, and short summaries of readings, as well as more formal writing, such as critical responses to readings and revisions of drafts.

The chapters in Unit One introduce students to the strategies they will use in the other units. The students are asked to read some short academic texts, but most of their writing in Unit One centers on their own experiences. We've begun the book this way to enable students to begin writing from their strengths and to help them build self-assurance as writers. Unit One also introduces students to strategies for developing notes and drafts into revised and edited essays. All of these strategies are used in the other units, where the students read short passages, take notes, discuss the readings, write drafts from their notes and the discussions, comment on one anothers' drafts, and revise and edit their writing. Units Two, Three, and Four, are each centered on a different academic content area: social sciences, applied sciences, and humanities.

Writing in the Content Areas

Non-native college students who take ESL classes either are concurrently enrolled in or are planning to be enrolled in content courses that are part of their major or distribution requirements. In these courses they must read textbooks, take notes from lectures and readings, discuss ideas, take exams, and write papers. They therefore need plenty of practice reading academic texts and discussing and writing about those texts to increase their understanding. In *Academic Writing Workshop II* we provide this type of practice, focusing on different content areas of the social sciences, the applied sciences, and the humanities. Because this is not a reading book, we have chosen short academic texts for the students to read and have asked them to write extensively about these texts. Some of the writing is speculative and informal; other writing is more formal, having gone through revision and editing.

Writing as a Tool for Learning

The writing assignments in *Academic Writing Workshop II* are designed to help students understand the academic subject matter presented in the readings and discussion questions. The writing functions as a tool for learning in the following ways: (1) it promotes greater interaction between ESL readers and the texts; (2) it leads to more focused and critical reading; (3) it provides starting points for more formal writing; and (4) it helps ESL students become more comfortable writers and more proficient users of English. We have included a variety of writing assignments, such as answering questions, mapping, and list making, that will help the students discover what they're thinking and then explore and develop these ideas. Other writing assignments (dialogue journal writing and double-entry notes) ask the students to engage in written conversations with peers or themselves about the topics under consideration, again with the aim of helping the students develop their thinking further.

Small Group Work

Along with reading and discussing texts and writing about them, students will work with one another in pairs or small groups. They will share and respond in their groups. *Sharing* is reading one's writing aloud to others, and *responding* is giving and receiving feedback about drafts-in-progress.

Small groups provide students with an audience for their writing-in-progress. Sharing provides them with the reassurance that their peers are struggling with writing as much as they. Each group member learns that writing is difficult for everyone. Small groups take student writers out of their isolation and bring them into contact with fellow writers who are also trying to fulfill assignments and develop their ideas in writing. The size of the groups is flexible, depending on the total number of students in the class and the time available for work. Three to five students is a good size for a group when any sharing of writing is involved. Although we often specify small group work, feel free to change the groupings, using, for example, pairs or the whole class in place of small groups.

Writing Assignments in This Book

Each chapter in this book includes Academic Journal, in-class, and at-home writing assignments.

The Academic Journal is not a journal in the traditional sense; that is, it is not a diary of intimate experiences. Instead, it is a notebook in which students write frequently for a variety of academic purposes without attention to correcting errors.

For students, the Academic Journal is a place to try out ideas in writing, jot down reactions to the class and the writing assignments, maintain an ongoing vocabulary list, take notes, and keep track of their own development as writers. For you, the Academic Journal is a monitoring device. Because you will periodically collect and read your students' Academic Journals, you will be able to check students' progress and respond to their writing.

And because you will comment in writing after some of the students' journal entries, you will engage in an ongoing, one-to-one dialogue with your students, a dialogue about ideas that is free from judgment and admonition about faulty language use. Instruct students to begin this dialogue with you by marking those entries they want you to read and respond to. Because Academic Journal writing serves to promote fluency, we caution against correcting the journal entries.

In this book, students are also instructed to do some writing in class and other writing at home. In-class writing assignments may be done at home, and at-home assignments may be done in class. Assignments requiring group work must be done in class.

We do, however, want to emphasize the importance of writing in class. It helps to counteract the loneliness of writing and should therefore be encouraged. Create a community of writers in the classroom by bringing in your own work-in-progress and by writing along with your students.

Writing Folder

As students complete in-class writing assignments, response sheets, and at-home writing assignments, they should place their work in a Writing Folder. Any kind of folder that is at least 8½ by 11 inches will do.

The Writing Folder will help students keep their work together and organized. Students should not throw away any of their writing; they should keep together everything that is related to one paper—drafts, notes, response sheets, and so on—in their Writing Folders. Students will occasionally turn in their folders to you for diagnosis, response, or evaluation, as indicated throughout this book.

Diagnosing Students' Writing Problems

Even before you receive Writing Folders from your students for the first time (Chapter 1), look for certain signs as you watch your students write in class. Does a student pause, cross out, or erase a lot? Does a student use the dictionary frequently? Does a student ask, "What should I write?" Is the student's paper noticeably shorter than classmates' papers? A combination of several of these signs may indicate writing anxiety.

The work in students' Writing Folders will help you complete your diagnoses. Here are some suggestions for what to look for as you read through their work:

—Level of language ability

—Comprehensibility

—Control of ideas

—Connectedness of ideas

—Inability to follow assignment directions (may indicate a reading problem)

—Length

—Problems with orthography

—Problems with spelling

—Recurring usage errors

Your in-class observations and assessment of students' early written work will help you determine what to work on in class to supplement the book's writing assignments and group work.

Responding to Students' Writing

Responding to students' writing may be the most demanding part of a writing teacher's job. Writing teachers want their comments to promote change and to encourage students to continue writing. ESL writing teachers feel extra responsibility because they believe they must deal simultaneously with their students' errors and ideas. The difficulty of their task makes writing teachers wish for a magic formula for responding to student writing that works every time for every student. Of course, such a formula does not exist. Each student's draft is unique, with its own set of strengths and weaknesses. Each student has his or her own abilities and needs. The teacher must take all these particularities into account when responding to a student's draft. Therefore, an all-purpose response strategy is impossible to construct.

Here, however, are some general guidelines to keep in mind as you respond to students' drafts-in-progress (we have indicated in the book when you are expected to respond).

—Tell the student what you understood from the draft. This will allow the writer to know what the writing communicated to a reader.

—Keep your comments "text-specific"; that is, refer to specific parts of the student's text. Comments such as "too general" and "unclear," for example, do not indicate which portion of the student's text might be perceived as too general or unclear and why. Even a positive comment such as "Great idea!" is not as helpful as one that also explains which idea seems so good and why.

—In early drafts, point out usage problems only when they interfere with meaning.

—Don't overwhelm students with too many comments. Keep the revising process manageable.

—Remember that once you have made your comments, it is the students' responsibility to act on them. Don't expect that they will incorporate all your comments in their revisions.

Usage Problems

In Chapter 3 the students begin to edit their writing. Because editing requires a different set of awarenesses than developing, organizing, and clarifying ideas in writing, we have created editing assignments that allow students to monitor their progress as editors. Thus, part of each student's

Academic Journal will become an "editing log," a record of errors and corrections that the student can add to and review.

Evaluating Student Writing

As they progress through the book, the students will evaluate their own work, either in letters to you included in their Writing Folders or in comments made in their Academic Journals. Then, at the end of each unit, they will select one of their revisions for you to grade. This arrangement forces the students to consider their progress as writers and also relieves you of the burden of evaluating everything they write. You do not need to implement any special system of evaluation. Most traditional methods of grading student writing—letter grades, percentages, pass/fail, and so on—can be easily integrated into the procedures specified in the chapters. We recommend, however, that you do not grade drafts-in-progress but evaluate only the final edited drafts of papers.

Examples of Student Writing

The examples of ESL student writing throughout this book are at a level of ability perhaps higher than you should expect from your own students. And you may find that your students don't write as much as appears in the longer examples. Please keep in mind, too, that except for the texts in the first unit (Chapters 1–3), which the students will be asked to read carefully and analyze for language errors, the student texts in the book have been edited to some degree.

Assignments are preceded by examples of student writing that were triggered by those assignments. These examples serve as models for the users of this book. You and your students will be instructed to read and discuss the models before students do the assignments.

Introduction to Students

Academic Writing

All students write. They take notes from readings and from lectures. They write summaries and essays. This writing is called "academic writing." Academic writing is sometimes called "writing to learn." When you take notes and write summaries and essays about history, biology, computer science, or English, you are writing in order to understand and learn the subject matter more fully.

Writing Process

The questions students ask most often about writing are:

—Where do I get ideas to begin writing?

—How can I continue writing?

—How can I complete and correct a piece of writing?

Academic Writing Workshop II will help you work on these questions by showing you ways to start writing, keep writing, read your writing, show your writing to other students and your teacher, talk about your writing, change your writing, and correct your writing. Notice that you will correct your writing at the *end* of this process.

How to Use This Book

Academic Writing Workshop II invites you to write in class and at home, for yourself, your teacher, and your classmates. You will keep an Academic Journal for some assignments and a Writing Folder for other assignments. Sometimes you will sit in a small group with other students and read your writing out loud. At other times, your teacher will read your writing and give you feedback. So, even though this is a writing textbook, you will have many opportunities to read, listen to, and talk about your own and other people's writing.

Throughout the book you will find examples of student writing. Some of these examples are notes or lists; others are uncorrected pieces of writing (drafts); others are finished and corrected pieces of writing (edited drafts). You will read these examples before you do your own in-class or at-home writing. The examples of student writing may give you ideas for doing your own writing.

Academic Writing Workshop II is divided into four units, Writing to Learn, Writing About Social Sciences, Writing About Applied Sciences, and Writing About Humanities. While working in the first unit, you will learn writing strategies that will help you understand what you are reading and studying in the other units. In each chapter, there are reading and writing assignments you will do in class or at home. In addition, in some chapters you will find charts, response sheets, and questionnaires. All of the assignments will be explained before you begin to write. You and your teacher will decide what order you want to follow in progressing through the book. But you should save the last chapter, "Publishing," for the end. It has instructions for how to put together a class magazine of student writing.

Please study the Table of Contents to find out how the units and chapters of this book are put together.

UNIT ONE

Writing to Learn

In the next three chapters you will practice some strategies for writing that will help you learn more about whatever topic you are studying. In Chapter 1, you will practice activities to help you understand what you know already. In Chapter 2, you will practice note taking, summarizing, and other activities to help you understand the things you read. In Chapter 3, you will begin revising and editing.

Writing About What You Already Know

In this chapter

—You will practice ways to discover what you know about a topic before you read about it, as well as ways to generate ideas for writing essays.

—You will begin an Academic Journal and a Writing Folder.

—You will begin two essays on different topics and evaluate your writing.

Words and Phrases to Watch For

Academic Journal	Expertise
Writing Folder	Mapping
Generating ideas	Drafting
Making lists	Recorder

Keeping an Academic Journal

In Class

Throughout this book, you will do a great deal of writing to help you think about academic subjects. You will do this writing in a notebook called an

demic Journal. Sometimes you will share this writing with your classes or your teacher, and they will write comments in your journal.
.re is no need to worry about writing correctly in your Academic Jour-
. You need only to be concerned with exploring your ideas through
.ting.

Make sure your name is on the front of your Academic Journal.
Open the journal to the first page, and put today's date at the top of
that page. (Be sure to put the date every time you write in your
Academic Journal.)

2. Spend about ten minutes writing an answer to the following
   question. This will be your first journal entry. Remember that you
   don't need to worry about spelling, punctuation, or grammar. Just
   write.

   What do I want to learn in this class?

3. Reread your answer to the question, and underline a phrase or a
   sentence you would like to read to the whole class. Share* the part
   you underlined with your classmates. Did anyone in the class have a
   similar answer?

Making Lists to Generate Ideas

At Home

Choose one of the topics below, and spend about twenty minutes writing
about it in your Academic Journal. Your teacher might want to add other
possible topics to the list.

1. Your autobiography as a learner of English

2. Your greatest success as a writer (in your first language or in English)

3. The things you worry about when you write in your first language or
   in English

Spend about ten minutes making two lists. First, list the subjects you
would like to write about during the next two or three weeks. Try to think
of at least five different topics. Then list your areas of expertise, that is,
the things you do well. These could be hobbies, a job, or anything else.
Try to think of at least two for this list.

---

* To share your writing means to read it aloud to a partner, a small group, or a class.

In his journal, Zheng wrote the following list of topics that he wanted to write about:

> My problems with English language
> Bicycle travel with work friends
> Working in Chinese restaurant

Zheng also wrote the following list of his areas of expertise:

> math
> Chinese language
> Chinese restaurants

With a partner, choose the topic or area of expertise from Zheng's journal that you think is the most interesting. Which one would you want to know more about? Explain your choice to the class.

In Class

In a small group, share the lists you made of subjects you would like to write about and your areas of expertise. Have your group members tell you which topic or expertise they would like you to write about. Ask them to explain their choice. Then, using your group members' suggestion, choose a topic or expertise from your list to write your first essay about. You'll begin writing it after you read more about Zheng's topic and essay.

From List to Draft

In Class

With the help of his group, Zheng decided to write about the bicycle trip he took with his fellow workers. On a blank page in his journal, he listed ideas and then used numbers to organize the ideas. His list follows:

> bicycle travel with friends
> 5. to country
> 3. every one bring somethings - fruit,
>   bread, 水桶 (bucket)
> 4. bicycle ride - pleasant
> 7. impress girlfriend

6. noises - talking, bicycles, things
8. enjoying - peacefulness
1. why - after period of hard work, reward
2. deciding

Discuss Zheng's list. What do you notice about it? How is this list different from his earlier one?

In Class

In your Academic Journal, make a list about the topic you chose. When you are finished, share your list with a partner, and ask your partner for suggestions about things to add to the list.

At Home

After brainstorming about his topic, Zheng wrote the following draft for his first essay:

Back to Nature

About 2 years ago, a trouble subject exhausted everyone of my task group. After it was completed, all of us had a same idea: to take a good rest. Most of us like to go out of door. We stayed the office each day for three months. We hated the office and were headache to the CRT. But where we should go? We discussed this problem for long time. Some people said there and there are better, but some said not. That's no easy to find out a place everybody satisfy. Anyway, we found a place after all. But I didn't think there was better. I couldn't imagine that anything would be interesting. But I had to agree with them. The place we plan to go was settle down. Next was preparing. We had to take woods as fuel. We had to buy soom foods. And we had to borrow two or three hunting guns for those unfortunate birds. After two day's preparing everything were ready. We had one day off per week. We had to listen to radio in order to know the weather of the day we do and made sure it would be nice.

That day I got up early, about 5:30, and brought goods what they wanted me to do. Some fruids, bread, and a small bucket. I was on time. All of us except a trouble guy were on time too. We waited twenty minutes because his losing bicycle's key. I remember there always were glad laugh with the wonderful music of spoons to tought bucket when we rode each own bicycle. I felt the air was so fresh, the mountains was so green, and the sky was so blue. Everything was wonderful. I forgot all of unhappiness and disorder. First time I found that we lived on such beautiful nature. We arrived after one and half hours riding. I took a hunting gun and I couldn't wait everything putting down. I was crazy about hunting. I remember I was very glad because didn't missing the first shot. We had very wonderful lunch. After the lunch. We made a circle playing game. The programs were interesting. Everybody could order anyone to plan any program. I ordered the trouble-man to put his head into water for 10 minutes and he really did. He was a man. I knowed he is advanced in swimming and he like to show himself. There were so many funny programs. But I cann't remember all of circumstances and I don't know how to describe it. Indeed, it was better than I suppose before.

Honestly, I really don't like the rural life. I like to back to nature and love nature very much.

In the space below, write your comments about Zheng's draft: What do you like about it? What additional information would you like Zheng to include? What information do you think he can omit? Are there any parts of Zheng's essay you don't understand? What other questions do you have for Zheng?

In Class

Use the following procedure to share your comments about Zheng's draft with your classmates. Then discuss this draft and the list Zheng made before he wrote it.

1. Choose a recorder to write the various comments on the blackboard. Read some of your comments to the class. Did other students agree with you? Did anyone disagree with you? Did other students notice good parts or problems in Zheng's draft that you had missed?

2. Compare Zheng's draft with his second list. What parts of the list did he omit in his draft? What parts of the draft are not included in the list? How did he organize his draft? Do you think he made the right choices?

At Home

Look at the list about the topic for your first essay, and use it to help you write a draft. You might want to number the items to help you with organization. When you have finished writing this draft, answer the following questions on an extra sheet of paper, and attach this page to your draft.

Self-Evaluation Questions

1. What was I trying to say in this draft?

2. Am I happy with what I wrote?

3. What did I have problems with?

4. What parts of my draft need more work?

In Class

Exchange your draft with a partner. Read your partner's draft, and fill out Response Sheet A. When your partner returns your draft, read the response and ask him or her about any comment you don't understand.

Keeping a Writing Folder

For this class you will keep all your loose papers in a Writing Folder, which your teacher will collect periodically to read, comment on, and evaluate your writing. All notes, drafts, response sheets, and evaluations for a particular essay should be stapled or clipped together. Your teacher will want to trace the development of your essays from rough notes to final draft, and you too will want to review your work at times.

Clip together the draft, self-evaluation, and response sheet you have just finished working on, and put these in your Writing Folder. Make sure that all pages have your name on them and that everything is dated.

Mapping to Generate Ideas

In Class

Mapping is similar to making a list, but in mapping you use circles and lines to show connections and relationships between ideas. The following is an example of mapping that a group of students did on "Living Alone."

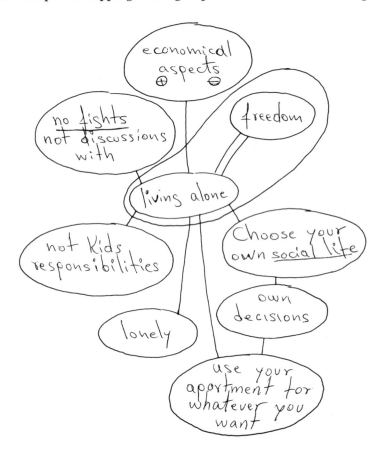

Discuss with your classmates how this map is different from Zheng's list on pp. 6–7. How is this kind of map similar to or different from a geographical map? In small groups, choose someone to be the recorder, and do a group map on the following topic:

How is your life different now from your parents' lives when they were your age?

You may want to start your map with two centers: one for your parents and one for you.

Response Sheet A: First Essay

Your name _____

The writer's name _____

Date _____

1. What is this essay about?

2. What do you like about this essay? Why?

3. What parts (if any) confuse you?

4. What questions do you have for the writer?

Tear out this sheet, and return it with the draft to the writer.

When you are finished, draw your group's map on the blackboard, and explain it to the rest of the class. Compare the various maps. In what ways do they look similar or different? What similar information do they have? What different information do they have?

From Map to Draft

At Home

Review the lists of subjects and expertises you made in your Academic Journal and choose another one to write about. (If you didn't write about one of your expertises for the last essay, try to choose one for this essay.) On a loose sheet of paper, spend about thirty minutes doing a map for this new topic. When you have finished doing the map, write briefly in your Academic Journal about the map: Describe the map, and explain briefly what you would like to say about this topic.

In Class

Share your map and journal entry about the map with a partner, and place the map in your writing folder. You'll write a draft about this topic after you read about Virginie's draft.

At Home

Virginie decided to write about making friends, one of her expertises. Virginie's map and journal entry follow. Read them carefully, and in the space below, write down any questions you have about the map or entry.

how to make friends

what kind the person am I

what are the required qualities for a person might have. to be my friend

help

sadness

accept

joy

defect

boyfriend

how do I know that a person can be my friend

understanding

marriage

smile

listening

fun

sympathetic

open

In my map I am showing that I can find a friend.
I want a friend is sympathetic, open, fun, etc. I must
to be patient with my friend's problems. There is sadness,
and also there is happiness. Friends can fall in love,
therefore friends can be married. Making friends is not
difficult, I can tell people "how to make friends."

Virginie met with a partner to discuss her map and journal entry, and
she took the following brief notes on her partner's comments and questions.

— is it really easy? Yes

people afraid to try to
make friends — why?

If you
Know
how

attracting — when someone smiles at you

↳ maybe a good friend

After her discussion with her partner, Virginie reviewed her map, journal entry, and notes, and she wrote the following draft. Read the draft carefully. How do you think she used her map and notes to write her draft?

Most of people have the difficulty to have friends because they think that nobody can not accept them as friends or they are too shy, or too scared to try an experience with some one.

A person who needs to make friends have to be open to every one, it is not mean that every body is going to be his friend, but he will have at least the opportunity to choose. First of all, a smiling person is attracting, and it shows that he has a lot of sunshine in his life, therefore, many people want to take advantage of it. Another thing which can be attractive to others is, wether you have the faculty to accept others like they are, with their qualities and defects, listen to them because in those day, people need to be listened and understood, try to work out problems with them.

In order to keep up this relationship a person has also to be willing to get fun with others, to share their happiness as he shares his sadness. I am sure from this experience, many things can happen such as, a man and a woman can fell in love to each other and got married later. We also know that many times our friends help us more than our parents did, so, nobody should not be scared to approached others, or shyness maybe has to be eliminated in our life.

So it's easy to make friends, and it is important for us because we are part of the society, we can not ignore it, therefore, we have to do something in order to feel comfortable, and having friends is a step to take.

In the space below, write a brief response to Virginie's draft. Comment on the parts you liked (and why) and on the parts that confused you, and list any questions you have.

In Class

Share your response about Virginie's draft with the class. How does your response compare to those of your classmates? Discuss the differences and similarities between Virginie's draft and her map. Do you think she made good choices in what she included and what she omitted? Does the organization of her draft make sense to everyone in the class?

At Home

Review your map, journal entry, and discussion notes, and use these to help you write a draft of your second essay. On another sheet of paper, answer the following questions about your draft.

Self-Evaluation Questions

1. What was I trying to say in this draft?

2. Am I happy with what I wrote?

3. What did I have problems with?

4. What parts of my draft need more work?

In Class

Exchange your draft with a partner. Read your partner's draft carefully, and comment on your partner's draft, using Response Sheet B. When your partner returns your draft with his or her response, read it carefully and ask about any comment you don't understand. Clip or staple everything together, and put it in your Writing Folder.

At Home

Write a brief letter to your teacher about what you have learned so far in the class. Discuss the drafts you wrote; the various activities with your partner, a small group, or the whole class; and the Academic Journal. Make sure the letter is dated, sign it, and put it in your Writing Folder. Your teacher will collect the folder, read your letter and your two sets of notes and drafts, and respond to your work before returning the Writing Folder to you.

At Home

Look at the words and phrases at the beginning of this chapter, and write them in your Academic Journal. What do they mean? Write the definition next to each word or phrase.

Response Sheet B: Second Essay

Your name _____

The writer's name _____

Date _____

1. What is this essay about?

2. What do you like about this essay? Why?

3. What parts (if any) confuse you?

4. What questions do you have for the writer?

Tear out this sheet, and return it with the draft to the writer.

Summary

In this chapter you began your Academic Journal and Writing Folder, you learned about listing and mapping, you wrote drafts of two essays, and you responded to two drafts. In Chapter 2 you will learn about taking two kinds of notes: dialogue and double-entry. Both are ways to use writing to learn.

Writing About What You Are Learning

In this chapter

—You will learn ways to use writing to help you understand anything you are studying.

—You will study two ways to take notes.

—You will begin two writing assignments based on articles.

—You will evaluate your writing.

Words and Phrases to Watch For

Dialogue notes   Double-entry notes

Response   Opinion

Note taking

Dialogue Notes

In Class

A paragraph from a history textbook* and the entry that a student (Milton) wrote about the paragraph in his Academic Journal follow. Milton's teacher had asked him to address the following questions:

---

*From *War* by Gwynne Dyer © 1985 by Business Media Resources. Used by permission of Crown Publishers, Inc., and Knox Burger Associates, Ltd.

1. What was difficult to understand about this paragraph?

2. What is your opinion about the writer's ideas?

3. What questions do you want to ask during the class discussion?

4. How would you summarize this paragraph (in one or two sentences)?

The government and society of the United States are greatly different from those of the Soviet Union or Egypt, but their armies are so close in structure and in spirit that their officers, when they come into contact, cannot help recognizing their common membership in a single, universal profession whose characteristics everywhere are shaped by the demands of battle. Not only the system of military rank but all the most striking characteristics of armies— the rote learning and standardization, the seemingly contradictory emphases on strict obedience and individual initiative (both of which may be described as "heroism," depending on the circumstances), even their typical social conservatism—are intimately connected with the fact that armies are in the business of imposing order upon chaos, and of forcing men to do what they very much do not want to do. The key problem in fighting a battle has always been control: he who is less badly informed and less disorganized wins. (p. 133)

Milton's entry follows:

1. We have to read slowly, and we can understand its meaning, but not all
2. The ideas in some sentences goes straight to the point, although there are some empty spaces missunderstandable.
3. What about the power (in refference with information and organization, at the end).
4. governments and society are differents with other countries armies are the same in structure and spirit shaped by the demands of battle.

What do you notice about Milton's entry? How does it differ from underlining or highlighting phrases in the paragraph?

Milton exchanged his journal with Tony, who wrote the following comment under Milton's entry:

I think that you mean by power, that the author forget to write down that besides good organization and been well informed happens to be that the more strong and powerful army usually wins. Isn't it?

21

Talking about structure and organization. I think that different countries adopt the best ways they can in training their armies. In this case I think that so many countries adopted the German discipline and order to train their armies.

You'll let me know if I'm wrong.

What do you notice about Tony's comment? How do you think this comment will help Milton understand the paragraph better? Why do you think these are called "dialogue" notes?

At Home

Read the following paragraphs.*

Islam is not a religion and Muhammad is not the founder of Islam. This may seem a statement of extreme Islamic heresy. Yet this is not too far from what two fundamentalist Islamic scholars and reformers have to say about the basic tenets of their faith: "Islam is not a religion in the common, distorted meaning of the word, confining itself to the private life of man. It is a complete way of life, catering for all the fields of human existence. Islam provides guidance for all walks of life—individual and social, material and moral, economic and political, legal and cultural, national and international." These words are echoed by every writer, Muslim or non-Muslim, dealing with the most essential characteristic of this faith, a characteristic which it does not share with any of the other "higher religions."

Because of this it cannot be repeated too often that Islam is "not merely a religion." It is a total and unified way of life, both religious and secular; it is a set of beliefs and a way of worship; it is a vast and integrated system of law; it is a culture and a civilization; it is an economic system and a way of doing business; it is a **polity** and a method of **governance**; it is a special sort of society and a way of running a family; it prescribes for inheritance and divorce, dress and etiquette, food and personal hygiene. It is a spiritual and human totality, **this**-worldly and **other**-worldly. (p. 17)

In your Academic Journal, answer the following questions about these paragraphs:

1. What was difficult to understand about these paragraphs?

2. What is your opinion about the writer's ideas?

---

*From G. H. Jansen, *Militant Islam* (New York: Harper & Row, 1980).

3. What questions do you want to ask during the class discussion?

4. How would you summarize these paragraphs (in one or two sentences)?

In Class

Exchange journals with a partner, and read your partner's entry on these paragraphs. Write dialogue notes in your partner's journal about his or her entry. Try to answer your partner's questions or explain what his or her entry made you think about. Return the journal to your partner and read his or her dialogue notes about your entry. With your partner, choose one question to ask the class. Discuss the passage with the whole class.

Writing a Draft from Dialogue Notes

At Home

After his class discussed the first passage, Milton reread his journal entry and wrote a response to summarize his opinions and questions about the paragraph. His draft follows. Read it carefully, and in the space that follows it, write some comments about how this draft is different from and similar to Milton's journal entry.

The author, in this article is trying to describe what an army is. He said that an army, from their roots until the purpose for which it was created, is the same in all place. Begining with their officers of highest rank until the soldiers of lowest rank. There is not difference between them do not matter the country, religion status, or political regiment.

The author said, "The armies are in the business of imposing order upon chaos." In some cases it is true, but in most of them the armies are used by the politicians to do what they want to do.

At the end of the article the author wrote, "He who is less badly informed and less disorganized wins". Probably that should be true, but in the armies business I don't know anything about that. I personally believe that the author forgot to includ something about the powerful. I think, that in some cases the powerful of an army has to play a very importan role.

In the same sentence, I understand that both armies are bad in the problem of fighting a battle, and win from the bad the less bad.

That make me believe that the author is not agree with the idea of armies and wars. I would like to say, that I am not agree with wars an armies too.

Your comments about Milton's draft:

In Class

Share your comments about Milton's draft with your classmates. Did others in the class have similar comments? Did they notice anything in the draft that you did not notice?

At Home

Reread your journal entry about the second passage, including your partner's dialogue notes about your entry. Then, using either listing or mapping, generate some ideas for a short response essay, in which you'll explain your opinions and questions about the paragraphs. When you have finished writing this draft, answer the following questions on a separate sheet of paper.

Self-Evaluation Questions

1. What did I want to say about the paragraphs?

2. Was I successful?

3. What did I have problems with?

4. What parts of my draft need more work?

Attach the self-evaluation to your draft, and bring them both to class.

In Class

Exchange your draft with a partner. Read your partner's draft carefully, and fill out Response Sheet C. When you have finished, return everything

Response Sheet C: Response Essay 1

Your name

The writer's name

Date

1. What was the writer's opinion about this article?

2. What were the writer's questions?

3. What did you find interesting about the writer's draft?

4. How did reading this draft help you understand the paragraphs better?

Tear out this sheet, and return it with the draft to the writer.

to your partner. Read your partner's comments on your own essay, and ask him or her about anything you don't understand. Staple or clip everything together, make sure that everything is dated, and place it all in your Writing Folder.

At Home

In your Academic Journal, write a summary of what you have learned so far in this chapter. Write more dialogue notes on one passage in the Appendix of this book, and exchange them with other students. What effect does this writing have on your understanding of the material?

Note Taking

In Class

Below are examples of ways to take notes on something you are reading.* Look over the examples carefully, and discuss their differences and similarities. Which method do you think is most effective? Why? What is the purpose of taking notes?

Example 1

The counting frame or **abacus** was a very early achievement of mankind. It follows the megalithic culture routes all round the world. The Mexicans and Peruvians were using the abacus when the Spaniards got to America. The Chinese and the Egyptians already possessed the abacus several millennia before the Christian era. The Romans took it from the Etruscans. Till about the beginning of the Christian era, this fixed frame remained the only instrument for calculation that mankind possessed.

To us, figures are symbols with which sums can be done. This conception of figures was completely foreign to the most advanced mathematicians of ancient Greece. The ancient number scripts were merely labels to record the result of doing work with an abacus, instead of doing work with a pen or pencil. In the whole history of mathematics there has been no more revolutionary step than the one which the Hindus made when they invented the sign "0" to stand for the empty column of the counting frame. (pp. 38–39)

---

*The paragraphs are from Lancelot Hogben, *Mathematics for the Million* (New York: Norton, 1983).

Example 2

The counting frame or **abacus** was a very early achievement of mankind. It follows the megalithic culture routes all round the world. The Mexicans and Peruvians were using the abacus when the Spaniards got to America. The Chinese and the Egyptians already possessed the abacus several millennia before the Christian era. The Romans took it from the Etruscans. Till about the beginning of the Christian era, this fixed frame remained the only instrument for calculation that mankind possessed.

[handwritten margin note:] abacus is important

To us, figures are symbols with which sums can be done. This conception of figures was completely foreign to the most advanced mathematicians of ancient Greece. The ancient number scripts were merely labels to record the result of doing work with an abacus, instead of doing work with a pen or pencil. In the whole history of mathematics there has been no more revolutionary step than the one which the Hindus made when they invented the sign "0" to stand for the empty column of the counting frame.

[handwritten margin note:] they didn't always used numbers.

Double-Entry Notes

Virginie, after reading the same passage, used a method called "double-entry notes," which she wrote in her Academic Journal. While reading, she marked the phrases and sentences she thought were important. After reading, she folded a page down the middle, and in the left-hand column wrote down the words, phrases, and sentences she marked in the story. In the right-hand column, she commented on the words, phrases, and sentences. Read her entry, and discuss how it compares with the preceding examples of note taking.

At Home

Choose one of the texts you haven't read from the Appendix, and make checks (√) while you are reading it. Write double-entry notes on it in your Academic Journal. You should spend at least twenty minutes doing the double-entry notes.

megalithic culture	can you say what is all about?
this conception of figures was completely foreign to the most advanced mathematicians of Ancient Greece	Should you not describe how the conception of figures became familiar to the mathematicians. What made them understand them? Is there an explanation for that? Because Mathematic seem to be abstract to many people. (For example can the mathematicians demonstrate why the formular of A + 2Ab + b, where did they find it, why is it like that.)
In the whole history of mathematics There has been no more revolutionary step than the one which the Hindus made when they invented the sign "0" . . .	Why since the revolutionary step that the Hindus made, there has been no more? If is because it's perfect or It is because they stop making progress or I donot Know ? what's going on!
	I like the last sentence of the first paragraph because it is pretty clear, gives an explanation of, in which way they used it.

Writing a Draft from Double-Entry Notes

At Home

After taking double-entry notes on the passage about mathematics, Virginie wrote the following explanation. She tried to keep in mind that she was writing for someone who might not know much about math. Read her explanation, writing your comments or questions in the margin.

If we take a look to the history of mathematics, we can see that one of the early instruments used for counting arround the world and by different countries have been the "Abacus." A particular characteristic of this device is that one of the columns—each column have units except one—is empty. It's a curious characteristic because this meant for the early users what means "zero" for us. However the ancient Hindus made the what we think the most revolutionary invention in the whole history of mathematic the sign "O" which stands for the empty column of the abacus. Since then mathematics took a gigantic advancement.

In Class

Share your comments about Virginie's draft with the class, and discuss her draft. How is it different from and similar to her notes? Do you think she has clearly explained what she has read? What other information do you think she needs to add?

At Home

Review your double-entry notes about the text from the Appendix. Using your notes, write a draft explaining this particular text to someone who hasn't read it. Then answer the following questions about it.

Self-Evaluation Questions

1. What was I trying to say in this draft?

2. Am I happy with what I wrote?

3. What did I have problems with?

4. What parts of my draft need more work?

Attach the self-evaluation to the draft.

In Class

Exchange your draft with a partner who didn't read the passage you read and wrote about. Read your partner's draft carefully, and respond to it, using Response Sheet D. Comment on any sections of the draft that are unclear or confusing to you. Then return everything to your partner, and read your partner's comments on your own essay. Ask him or her about any comment you don't understand. When you have finished talking with your partner, staple or clip the draft, self-evaluation, and response sheet together and place them in your Writing Folder.

At Home

Write a letter to your teacher about what you have learned from doing the activities in this chapter. Comment on the ways to take notes on and write a draft about a text. Also comment on the process of sharing your writing with others and responding to their writing. Date and sign this letter, and put it in your Writing Folder. Your teacher will collect the folder and respond to or evaluate all the new materials you have put in it for this chapter.

At Home

Look at the words and phrases at the beginning of this chapter, and write them in your Academic Journal. What do they mean? Write the definition next to each word or phrase.

Summary

In this chapter you took notes on and wrote about various texts. You learned how to take double-entry and dialogue notes, and you wrote two drafts. In Chapter 3 you will learn about revising and editing, and you will choose two drafts from your Writing Folder to revise and edit.

Response Sheet D: Response Essay 2

Your name

The writer's name

Date

1. What is the subject of the writer's draft?

2. What do you think is the most important point in the draft?

3. What do you like about this draft?

4. What questions do you have about this draft?

Tear out this sheet, and return it with the draft to the writer.

CHAPTER 3

Revising and Editing What You Have Written

In this chapter

—You will read about how one student revised a draft.

—You will revise two drafts in your Writing Folder.

—You will learn some editing strategies and edit your revisions before handing them in to your teacher for evaluation.

Words and Phrases to Watch For

Revising	Reorganization
Addition	Editing
Substitution	Strategies
Deletion	Editing log

What Is Revising?

To revise a draft means to change it, and there are many ways to change a draft. You can add or take out ideas, you can reorganize ideas, and you can change ideas. People revise to make their drafts easier to understand. Zheng revised his draft about his bicycle trip to the country, using the comments from his partner to help him decide what to add, take out, reorganize, or change.

In Class

Reread Zheng's draft about his bicycle trip (p. 7), and then read the following comments that Zheng's partner, Milton, wrote on the response sheet. In a small group, discuss how you think Zheng will be able to use Milton's comments to help him revise.

Milton's comments:

1. What is this essay about?

this essay is talking about a preparation and a trip to the nature, to the forest.

2. What do you like about this essay? Why?

I like the order, and details. Because it is describing step by step how things were or better how the things happened.

3. What parts (if any) confuse you?

the sentences--"All of us except a trouble guy were on time too." "There were so many funny programs" "I remember there always were glad laugh with the wonderful music of spoons to tought bucket when we rode each own bicycle."

4. What questions do you have for the writer?

What means a "CRT"?
What kind of programs the writer is talking about?

At Home

The first five paragraphs of Zheng's revision of his draft about the bicycle trip to the country with his fellow workers follow. Read the revision carefully, and compare it with his draft. How are they similar? How are they different? Which is better? Why? Write your answers to these questions, as well as any other comments, in the space below Zheng's revision.

Back to Nature

About 2 years ago, I worked in a software group of a microcomputer factory, China. There were twelve people in the group, five girls and seven boys, all about 23 years old.

A trouble subject with respect of forest source statistics exhausted everyone of us. It took us three months for the programming dealing with large amount of date. We were working in the offices everyday for the duration. And most of time we were in front of the CRT, the monitors of microcomputer. So, after it was completed, all of us had a same idea: to take a good rest. Most of us liked to go out of doors, only one suggested to go to a restaurant to have a rich meal. Of course, the hungry man only obeyed the others. But where we should go? Where is attractive? We discussed the problem for long time. Some people said where is better but some thought not. That's so difficult to find a place everybody satisfy. Anyway, we found a place after all. Then, I didn't think there was better. I couldn't imagine that anything would be interesting. I felt better after they told me that I could hunt birds there.

The second problem was when we should act. We only had one day off perweek. We couldn't prepare everything and put them in the office a week. The weather was the most important. Nobody like to go out of doors with umbrella. We listened to the radio about the weather forecast, although we didn't very believe it. We settled down when we would go.

The third problem was preparing. We took two days for it. We took some woods as fuel, bought foods and fruits, and borrowed two hunting guns for those unfortunate birds.

That was a day of later of the April. I got up early, about 5:30, and brought goods what they wanted me to do, some fruits, bread, and a small bucket. I was on time. All of us except a trouble guy were on time, too. But we waited twenty minutes because of finding his lost bicycle's key. We talked and laughed as we rode our bicycles. Our laughter mix with the wonder music of the spoons clanging inside the buckets. I talked with my girlfriend. I just remember that she asked me "why don't change a new shirt" and I answered "I don't think it's very important", immediately, I change other topic. I felt the air was so fresh, the mountains were so green, the sky was so blue, and breeze was so great. We rode by a wide river. There were some small boats on it. That was a picture. That was better by far than a picture. First time I found that we lived on such beautiful nature. I forgot all of unhappiness and disorder. I hoped the riding to keep going.

Write your comments here:

In Class

In a small group, compare Zheng's draft with his revision, and list the types of changes he made. Use the following four categories to help you list the changes:

Addition   *Substitution*   *Deletion*   *Reorganization*

Share your comments about Zheng's revision with your classmates. How did he use his partner's comments to revise? Did the other groups notice any changes your group had missed? As a class, evaluate the revision:

Which changes were good and which ones were not good? Why? Which version of Zheng's essay do most of your classmates like better? Why?

In your Academic Journal, write a brief definition of revision. Share this definition with your classmates, and try to come up with a definition the whole class can agree on. Copy the agreed on definition in your Academic Journal.

Revise a Draft

At Home

Look through your Writing Folder, and choose one draft to revise. Then use the following procedure.

1. Read your draft and your answers to the self-evaluation questions. Then read the response sheet from your partner and any comments from your teacher, and underline or highlight anything that seems important to you.

2. On a separate sheet of paper, write briefly about how you plan to revise your draft. Consider the following questions:

   What do I want to add?

   What do I want to delete?

   What do I want to reorganize?

   What do I want to change (substitute)?

3. Reread your draft, making notes in the margin about the changes you would like to make. If you are going to make big changes, you might want to draft these on a separate sheet of paper.

4. Recopy your draft, incorporating the changes you have decided to make. Then reread your revision, marking places where you are still not satisfied with what you have written. (Don't worry about correcting mistakes; you will do that later in the editing section.) You might want to revise again. When you are satisfied with everything, make a neat copy (be sure to skip lines) of the revision, and staple or clip everything together (including all your notes and intermediate drafts). Make sure that everything is dated, and write "Revision" at the top of the neat copy.

5. Using the chart on p. 41, make a brief list of the changes you made when you revised, with the reasons for the changes. When you have finished, attach this chart to your revision and place everything in your Writing Folder.

In Class

In your Academic Journal, spend about fifteen minutes writing about the process of revision. Consider the following questions:

—Was it easy or difficult for me to revise my draft? Why?

—What did I enjoy about doing the revision?

—What did I not like about doing the revision?

—What suggestions do I have for myself for the next revision?

Share some of your answers with your classmates and discuss the difficulties of revising. Try to give suggestions that will help make revising easier.

Revise Another Draft

At Home

Look through your Writing Folder, and choose a second draft to revise. Then use the same procedure you used to revise your other draft (p. 39). In your Academic Journal, write briefly about this second revision. Consider the following questions:

—Are you satisfied with your revision? Why or why not?

—Is the revision better than the draft? Why or why not?

—Is revising becoming easier for you? Why or why not?

What Is Editing?

Editing is not the same as revising. When you revise, you pay attention to the ideas in your drafts, trying to make them clear and well organized. When you edit, you pay attention to the language in your drafts, trying to make it correct. As you do the various assignments in this book, you will edit some of them. At the end of the book, you will choose one of your edited drafts to include in a class magazine.

In Class

On page 43 is a paragraph from Zheng's revision, with the editing marks and corrections he made. Read it over carefully. Were all his corrections good ones? Did he miss any mistakes? Did he make any corrections that confuse you? Discuss your evaluation of Zheng's editing with your classmates.

List of Revisions

Name

Date

Title or topic of essay revised

Change   *Reason for Change*

Addition:

Deletion:

Substitution:

Reorganization:

Comments:

Tear this sheet out, and attach it to your revision.

difficult

A trouble subject with respect of forest source statistics exhausted

everyone of us. It took us three months for the programming dealing

data

with large amount of date. We were working in the offices everyday

the

for the duration. And most of time we were in front of the CRT, the

monitors of microcomputer. So, after it was completed, all of us had a

same idea: to take a good rest. Most of us liked to go out of doors, only

of us

one suggested to go to a restaurant to have a rich meal. Of course, the

we *what place*

hungry man only obeyed the others. But where we should go? Where

a

is attractive? We discussed the problem for long time. Some people

what place

said where is better but some thought not. That's so difficult to find a

place everybody satisfy. Anyway, we found a place after all. Then, I

that place

didn't think there was better. I couldn't imagine that anything would

be interesting. I felt better after they told me that I could hunt birds

there.

In Class

Two paragraphs from Milton's response article (p. 23) follow. With a partner, read the article and correct the errors you find.

The author, in this article is trying to describe what an army is. He

said that an army, from their roots until the purpose for which it

was created, is the same in all place. Beginning with their officers of

highest rank until the soldiers of lowest rank. There is not difference between them do not matter the country, religion status, or political regiment.

In the same sentence, I understand that both armies are bad in the problem of fighting a battle, and win from the bad the less bad. That make me believe that the author is not agree with the idea of armies and wars. I would like to say, that I am not agree with wars an armies too.

With your partner, answer the following questions about editing Milton's paragraphs.

Editing Log: Milton's Paragraphs

1. To edit Milton's paragraphs, what did we do first?

2. How many times did we read Milton's paragraphs?

3. How much time did we need to edit Milton's paragraphs?

4. Did we disagree about any corrections? If so, what were they?

5. What mistakes did Milton make more than once?

In Class

Share your corrections and editing log with your classmates. Discuss whatever problems you had while editing Milton's paragraphs, and tell your classmates how you dealt with those problems.

Keeping an Editing Log

At Home

Begin your own editing log in a special section of your Academic Journal. You will need to reserve at least twenty-five pages for this section. On the first page of the log, write the date, and answer the following questions.

Self-Study: Editing

1. What are some of the mistakes you frequently make when writing?

2. How much time do you usually spend editing each piece of your writing?

3. What kinds of mistakes do you have problems finding?

4. Do you think you are a good editor? Why or why not?

Throughout this book, as you edit your work, you will write more in your editing log. You can use it as a place to list the errors you make frequently, as well as to keep notes on your teacher's comments about your writing.

Editing Your Own Writing

At Home

Use the following procedures to edit the revisions in your Writing Folder.

1. Choose one of the revisions in your Writing Folder. Spend at least twenty minutes editing it. Don't erase anything. Just draw a line through the mistake and write the correction above. Mark (*) any sentences, phrases, or words you are unsure of.

2. In your editing log, make a list of the errors you found and corrected, and mark (*) the corrections you are unsure of.

3. Repeat steps one and two for your other revision.

In Class

Exchange one of your edited revisions with a partner, and check your partner's revision. If you find a mistake your partner didn't find, underline it in pencil. When you have finished, talk to your partner about the mistakes you found in the revision. Help your partner with any corrections he or she is unsure of. Your teacher will help you and your partner with any problems.

At Home

Make a clean copy of your edited revision, including any corrections your partner made. Clip this copy together with all the notes and drafts, and put it in your Writing Folder. Your teacher will collect your Writing Folder to comment on your work.

Strategies for Editing

Good writers have strategies for finding the mistakes in their writing. Read the list below, and discuss it with your classmates. How many of these strategies do you use already? What other strategies can you add to the list?

1. Look for mistakes you repeat.

   Example: Check all verbs for the correct tense if you sometimes make verb tense mistakes.

2. Look for words that signal places where you sometimes make mistakes.

   Example: Check each sentence that begins with *Because* if you sometimes write fragments beginning with this word.

3. Underline words you are not sure how to spell, and look them up in a dictionary.

4. Locate and check all commas and connecting words if you tend to write long sentences.

5. Reread your editing log periodically.

6. Read your writing aloud to a partner, or listen to your partner read aloud to you. You will sometimes hear mistakes you couldn't see.

7. Ask for help from a native speaker.

Remember that asking for help with editing is not "cheating." Even professional writers have editors to help them correct their mistakes. As you do more editing, you will become a better editor; but in the meantime, don't hesitate to ask for help when you need it.

Unit Writing Folder Review

At Home

Reread all the work in your Writing Folder as well as all your journal entries. Write a letter to your teacher about the work you have done. Tell the teacher what you have learned about generating ideas, revising, and editing, and ask whatever questions you have. Choose one of your edited texts for your teacher to grade. Your teacher will collect your Writing Folder and respond to your letter, and he or she will also grade the text you chose.

At Home

Look at the words and phrases at the beginning of this chapter, and write them in your Academic Journal. What do they mean? Write the definition next to each word or phrase.

Summary

In this chapter you revised and edited two drafts from your Writing Folder, and you began an editing log in your Academic Journal. In Unit Two you will use all the strategies you learned in this unit to write about topics in the social sciences.

UNIT TWO

Writing About Social Sciences

In the next three chapters you will write about social change and its influence on people's expectations, attitudes, and behavior. In Chapter 4, you will write about the expectations people had before moving to a new country and the culture shock they experienced after arriving. In Chapter 5, you will write about attitudes toward languages and the people that speak them. In Chapter 6, you will write about changes in children's lives and child-rearing practices.

CHAPTER 4

Culture Shock

In this chapter

—You will study and write about your own and others' expectations before moving to the United States.

—You will write about the culture shock people experience when they first come to this country.

Words and Phrases to Watch For

Expectations	Prereading
Culture shock	Postreading
Excerpt	Melting pot
Observations	Ethnic

Expectations and Surprises

At Home

Complete the following sentences:

1. Before I came to the United States, I expected

2. When I first came to the United States I was most surprised by

In Class

Get into a group with three other students. Share the sentences you completed previously. All of the students should explain their answers. Fill in the following lists. Include answers from each group member.

Expectations We Had Before   *What Surprised Us When We Came*
Coming to This Country   *to This Country*

Compare your group's list with the other groups' lists. What are the similarities and differences?

At Home

Eleftheriou wrote a story about something that surprised him when he came to this country from Cyprus. His story follows. As you read, mark (√) places in the text you think are important or interesting.

Reality

May 9, 1986. Looking at New York from high was like a dream: towering skyscrapers, busy streets, parks, all packed together on a long, narrow island. Before I even "woke up," I found myself in front of the airport exit. I heard a voice calling my name. I looked around and saw my uncle fighting to reach me through the crowd. We walked to the car and started our trip to New Jersey.

I didn't know which way we were going. I was looking out of the window, watching things I had never seen before when I heard my uncle asking me to lock my door. When I asked why, the answer was, "We are in a very bad neighborhood."

The words "bad neighborhood" didn't mean anything to me. What was that? I looked out of the window once more, wondering what was wrong with that neighborhood. It was a very poor place, not crowded at all. The few people on the street were leaning against walls covered with paintings. There were policemen at every corner. It was, in short, the kind of neighborhood we usually find in "bad" movies.

My beautiful dream of New York had disappeared. In its place was a feeling of disappointment. I remember asking myself, is this America? In a country so powerful, so rich, are there people leading this kind of life, living in these kinds of places? People who today are alive and tomorrow.... who knows? Will my new home in New Jersey be like this?

The answer to that last question came when at last we arrived in Closter, New Jersey. A different view appeared in front of my eyes: private houses, woods, friendly people waving hello. I felt so relieved because I could live like a human.

As far as the other questions are concerned, I can't answer them. There are rich and powerful people, and poor and forgotten people. Both sides live their own lives, in their own world, with the poor maybe dreaming for a better life.

At Home

Reread Eleftheriou's story. In your Academic Journal, answer the following questions: What were Eleftheriou's expectations? What surprised him? How does his first day compare with your own?

In Class

1. Get into your writing group. Share the answers you wrote to the questions about Eleftheriou's story. How does Eleftheriou's first day in this country compare to those of the students in your group?

2. Look at the chart you filled out on p. 51. How were Eleftheriou's expectations and things that surprised him different from or similar to those of the students in your group?

Writing a Two-Part Story

At Home

Look at the two sentences you completed on pp. 50—51. Write a two-part story about (1) what you expected before coming to this country and (2) what surprised you when you came. After completing the draft, put it in your Writing Folder.

In Class

Bring the two-part story to class. Meet with a partner, and share your stories. Each of you will fill out Response Sheet E about your partner's draft.

Early and Later Observations

At Home

On the next few pages you will find excerpts from *Two Years in the Melting Pot* (San Francisco: China Books, 1984), by Liu Zongren, a Chinese journalist who moved to the United States (Chicago) in 1980 to study and learn about the culture. Before you begin to read, answer the following prereading questions in your Academic Journal. To answer them, you will have to use your imagination and your knowledge of what it's like to move to a new country.

1. What are some of the differences between Liu Zongren's country, China, and the United States?

2. What do you imagine he liked most about the United States?

3. What do you imagine he liked least about the United States?

At Home

Read the first excerpt. As you read, mark places in the text that you think are interesting or important.

First Excerpt

Here the author describes the first house he stayed in after arriving in Chicago.

Such a huge room for one person! Rich-colored drapes hung over the windows. A closet, a bureau, two tables and a big bed with a spring mattress. The bed sheets seemed light and silky. This would be the first time for me to sleep in such an elegant bedroom. I thought of Fengyun [his wife], how often she complained that our hard, board-bottomed bed was painful for her bad back. If at home we could have had such a bed with a spring mattress, she would certainly have felt better.

I counted six lights in the room—table lights, wall lights, even a bed light. Why would one person need so many lights? At home we had only one small light in each of our two bedrooms, and we didn't turn either one on until it was needed. . . . The day after I arrived, Mrs. McKnight gave me a tour of the house. Downstairs was the basement; the kitchen, living room, guest room and dining room were on the first floor; and on the second and third floors were bedrooms, half of which were unoccupied. We finished our tour back in the spacious kitchen. Mrs. McKnight opened the refrigerator, which was full of packages and bottles, and told me I was free to take out anything in it. I didn't know what the items in the refrigerator were or how to cook them, except for the eggs. In the corner of the room, she pointed out a line of bottles and said, "There is Coke and 7-Up over there. When you are thirsty, help yourself. There's ice in the freezer. If you would like beer to drink, tell John, and he will drive you to a liquor store." . . . I appreciated all she was offering me, but I wondered: why does a family of this size need to have so much food? (pp. 15–17)

Used by permission.

At Home

Reread the first excerpt. In your Academic Journal, take double-entry notes: Fold a page down the middle. In the left-hand column, write down the words, phrases, and sentences you marked in the story. In the right-hand column, write why you marked these words, phrases, and sentences. Explain why you think they are interesting or important.

In Class

Get into your writing group. Share your double-entry notes. Remember to take notes of the group discussion. What observations did Liu Zongren make during his first days in this country?

At Home

Read the following excerpts from *Two Years in the Melting Pot*. The second excerpt is from the middle of the book; the third is from the end. As you read, mark places in the text that you think are interesting or important.

Response Sheet E:
Expectations and Surprises

Your name

The writer's name

Date

1. What expectations did the writer have about the United States before coming here?

2. What surprised the writer about this country?

3. What do you like most about the story?

4. What, if anything, do you *not* understand?

Tear out this sheet, and return it with the draft to the writer.

Second Excerpt

As my American friends drove me around the city they always mentioned the racial and/or ethnic makeup of the people living in each area. Chicago, an international city, can be divided into pockets of Polish, Jewish, Mexican, Greek, Puerto Rican, and many other peoples. I could see the change in the ethnic and racial composition of Chicagoans whenever I rode the No. 49 bus along Western Avenue, the longest thoroughfare in Chicago. Going from north to south, I could not help noticing the changes in skin color of the boarding passengers—from whites to dark-skinned Latinos to blacks, with a mixture of yellows as we passed through the Chinatown area. I hated the No. 49 bus, not only because it was too slow—thirty minutes between runs—but because I didn't feel safe riding it. (p. 80)

Used by permission.

Third Excerpt

Most Chinese parents help their children select purchases. They love their children as much as any parent, and they like to buy things for them. After a Chinese mother has agreed to pay for an item, she lets her child make a choice. Then she says, "This one is no good," or "That one is better than this one." If the child insists on the one he or she has chosen and it is not to the liking of the mother, more often than not, the mother will refuse to buy the thing at all. Those mothers who give too much independence to their children are not considered good mothers by Chinese standards. "She spoils her son too much," her neighbors and colleagues will say.

I like the way American parents treat their children. The young ones are treated as small adults—that's why, I think, Americans are so much more independent than Chinese. In Chicago, I had noticed that parents often left their young children with baby-sitters while they went to a party or to the theater. Chinese parents seldom do that. I made a mental note that after I got back to China, I would give my son more freedom in deciding his own affairs. My wife is too dominating in this respect. I would persuade her to follow American parental practices. (pp. 189–190)

Used by permission.

In Class

Meet with your writing group. First, share your double-entry notes about the second and third excerpts. Next, ask your group members to help you choose some possible topics to write about from the right-hand column of your notes on excerpts one, two, and three. Write those topics in your Academic Journal.

At Home

Look at your list of possible writing topics about *Two Years in the Melting Pot*. Choose one topic. Spend fifteen minutes writing about why you chose this topic and what you would like to say in your essay.

In Class

Tell your group members which topic you chose, why you chose it, and what you would like to say in your essay. Ask your group members for feedback about your choice. Take notes on any suggestions they give you on what to include in your essay.

Writing a Draft from Notes

At Home

Review your double-entry notes, your group discussion notes, and your writing about your topic. Write a draft about your topic.

In Class

Share your draft with a partner. Have your partner fill out Response Sheet F. Read the response sheet, and ask your partner to explain anything you didn't understand. Listen to your partner's draft and fill out Response Sheet F. Put your draft and response sheet in your Writing Folder. Your teacher will collect your folder and respond to your draft.

At Home

Here are the questions you answered before reading the three excerpts. Answer them again in your Academic Journal. Then compare your prereading answers to your postreading answers.

1. What are some of the differences between Liu Zongren's country, China, and the United States?

2. What did he like most about the United States?

3. What did he like least about the United States?

In Class

Share your prereading and postreading answers with the whole class. Explain what differences you noticed between what you expected the excerpts to be about and what you discovered in reading them.

Response Sheet F: Observations

Your name _____

The writer's name _____

Date _____

1. What is this essay about?

2. What do you like about this essay? Why?

3. What parts (if any) confuse you?

4. What questions do you have for the writer?

Tear out this sheet, and return it with the draft to the writer.

At Home

Reread the two drafts you wrote in this chapter: the one about expectations and surprises and the one about the topic from your double-entry notes. Reread Response Sheets E and F, and read your teacher's comments. Then decide which of these two drafts you would like to revise. After choosing, use the following procedure:

1. Read your draft. Then read the response sheet from your partner and any comments from your teacher. Underline or highlight anything that seems important.

2. On a separate sheet of paper, write briefly about how you plan to revise your draft. Consider the following questions:

   What do I want to add?

   What do I want to delete?

   What do I want to reorganize?

   What do I want to change (substitute)?

3. Reread your draft, making notes in the margin about the changes you would like to make. If you are going to make big changes, you might want to draft these on a separate sheet of paper.

4. Recopy your draft, incorporating the changes you have decided to make. Then reread your revisions, marking places where you are still not satisfied with what you have written. You might want to revise again. (Don't worry about correcting mistakes; you will do that during editing in Chapter 6.) When you are satisfied with your writing, make a neat copy of the revision, and staple or clip everything together. Put all your notes and drafts in your Writing Folder.

In Class

In your Academic Journal, write a letter to your teacher explaining what you learned from reading the three excerpts and from writing about expectations and culture shock. Your teacher will collect your Academic Journal and respond to your letter.

At Home

Look at the words and phrases at the beginning of this chapter, and write them in your Academic Journal. What do they mean? Write the definition next to each word or phrase.

Summary

In this chapter you wrote about your own and other people's expectations, culture shock, and observations. In Chapter 5, you will write about attitudes toward and beliefs about using different languages.

Language and Society

In this chapter

—You will write about your own and others' attitudes toward and beliefs about the different languages spoken in the same country.

Words and Phrases to Watch For

Linguistic	Local
Chauvinism	Loyalty
Dialects	Official language
National	

Attitudes Toward Language

At Home

The following are statements about language. After reading each statement, circle "I agree" or "I disagree" and write a few sentences explaining why you agree or disagree, giving examples from your experience with using and learning languages.

1. All people who live in the same country should speak the same language.

   I agree / I disagree

2. Some languages have a more pleasant sound than others.

   I agree / I disagree

3. Some languages are superior to others.

   I agree / I disagree

In Class

Get into your group. Compare the explanations you and your group members wrote about why you agree or disagree with the three statements about language. Take notes during the discussion. Then write a group summary of what the members said about each statement.

Next, read the following explanations Tin wrote about the three statements. Discuss his responses with your group members: How do his responses compare to your group members' responses?

1. All people who live in the same country should speak the same language.

   (I agree) / (I disagree)

   I agree and I disagree because there should be a language for business and government, but in our homes and with our friends we like to speak our mother language.

2. Some languages have a more pleasant sound than others.

   I agree / (I disagree)

   I think if you like the person who speaks that language you're going to like the sound of the speaking. It depends on your attitude: if you hate those people, you hate the way they talk (it sounds bad to you).

3. Some languages are superior to others.
   I agree / I disagree ?

I don't know what means a "superior" language. Maybe some have more letters or words. They all have different pronunciation, grammar, vocabulary you have to study. So I can't write about some languages are superior to others.

Your group will now share its three summaries with the class. Take notes about the other groups' summaries. Discuss Tin's responses with the whole class.

Writing an Explanation

At Home

Choose one of the three statements about language. Use your group and class discussion notes to write an explanation of why some people agree and others disagree with that statement. Put your notes and explanation in your Writing Folder. Tin's explanation about the second statement follows. How is it different from his first response to the second statement?

Some people believe that French, Italian, Spanish and English are the most beautiful languages in the world, but I think they don't know the other languages. They only like those languages they can hear all the time on TV and the movies. When they hear language they never hear before, it sounds bad because they don't have that sound in their ear before. It sound funny.

If you speak a language that different from French, Italian, Spanish and English, you might feel embarass to speak it. Like in the college I never speak my language because the other people think it sounds unpleasant.

I think it depends on your attitude: if you like the person who speaks that language you're going to like the sound of the speaking. But if you hate that person, you're going to hate the way they talk. It sounds bad to you.

National and Local Languages

At Home

In the following paragraph from *Word Play*, Peter Farb discusses what he calls "linguistic chauvinism." Read the passage, and check any words or phrases you think are important.

A nation usually demands that its citizens express their loyalty to the state by speaking the single approved language. A government is suspicious even of dialects of its own language, because these appeal to local loyalties rather than to a single national loyalty. And as soon as a new nation is formed, it often attempts to adopt a national language that is exclusively its own. That happened after the American Revolution when several patriots urged that the new nation switch from English to Latin or even to some newly invented language. Noah Webster, however, stated in his *Dissertation on the English Language,* that he was willing to settle for an American form of English: "As a nation we have a very great interest in opposing the introduction of any plan of uniformity with the British language." (p. 158)

Reprinted by permission of Alfred A. Knopf, Inc.

At Home

In your Academic Journal, write a response to the paragraph by answering the following questions:

1. What was difficult to understand about this paragraph?

2. What is your opinion about the writer's ideas?

3. What questions do you have about the paragraph?

4. How would you summarize this paragraph (in one or two sentences)?

In Class

Exchange journals with a partner, and read your partner's entry on the paragraph. In your partner's journal, write a dialogue journal entry in response to his or her entry. Try to answer your partner's questions, or explain what his or her entry made you think about. Then return the journal to your partner, and read his or her response in your own journal.

At Home

Reread the paragraph. Then answer the following questions in your Academic Journal:

1. What is the national language of your country?

2. What are the local languages of your country?

3. What is the relationship of the national language to the local ones?

4. What do you believe *should* be the relationship between national and local languages?

In Class

Get into your group. Share your answers to the questions about national and local languages. Then fill out the following chart for the countries represented in your group:

Country   *National Language*   *Local Languages*   *Relationship*

Share this chart with the other groups. Discuss what you believe should be the relationship between national and local languages. Spend fifteen minutes writing in your journal about what you learned from the group and class discussions.

At Home

In this paragraph from the same chapter of *Word Play,* the author continues his discussion of attitudes toward national and minority languages. Read the passage.

To achieve a national language, the state often scorns those in its midst who speak minority languages. The ancient Greeks demeaned the foreigners whom they fought because, to superior Greek ears, foreign speech sounded like a stammering *bar-bar;* Genghis Khan's Mongolian hordes received their name "Tatars" from the Chinese, who thought their outlandish speech sounded like *ta-ta;* and "Hottentot" is a coinage by the South African Dutch to indicate their low opinion of native speech. The people of the Aztec Empire of Mexico called their language *nahuatl* which means "pleasant-sounding," but used the word nonotli, "stammering," to describe other languages. And so it has probably been since the first speech communities arose, each considering its tongue superior to that of its neighbors, or of the people it colonizes. (pp. 159–160)

Reprinted by permission of Alfred A. Knopf, Inc.

In your Academic Journal, answer the following questions about this paragraph:

1. What was difficult to understand about this paragraph?

2. What is your opinion about the writer's ideas?

3. What questions do you have about the paragraph?

4. How would you summarize this paragraph (in one or two sentences)?

In Class

Exchange journals with a partner, and read your partner's entry on the paragraph. In your partner's journal, write a response to his or her entry. Try to answer your partner's questions, or explain what his or her entry made you think about. Return the journal to your partner, and read his or her response in your own journal.

At Home

Reread the paragraph. Answer the following questions in your Academic Journal:

1. Have you ever reacted positively or negatively toward people who didn't speak your language? If so, who were the people, what were your reactions, and why did you have those reactions?

2. What have you noticed about attitudes toward minority languages in this country?

In Class

Get into your group. Share your answers to the questions about reactions and attitudes toward speakers of other languages. Spend fifteen minutes writing about what you learned from the discussion.

At Home

In your Academic Journal, make a list of the topics you have read about, discussed, and written about in this chapter. Look through your discussion notes, answers to questions, dialogue journal entries, and entries about what you learned. Choose one topic you would like to write about, and make a map of that topic. Write briefly in your Academic Journal about the map: Describe the map, and explain what you would like to say about the topic.

In Class

Share your map and journal entry about the map with your group members. Take notes on your group members' comments and questions about your map.

Writing a Draft from a Map

At Home

Review your map and group members' comments and questions, and use them to write a draft. On another sheet of paper, answer the following questions about your draft.

Self-Evaluation Questions

1. What was I trying to say in this draft?

2. Am I happy with what I wrote?

3. What did I have problems with?

4. What parts of my draft need more work?

In Class

Exchange drafts with a partner. Read your partner's draft, and comment on it, using Response Sheet G. When your partner returns your draft with his or her response, read it carefully, and ask about any comments you don't understand. Clip everything together, and put it in your Writing Folder. Your teacher will collect your folder, respond to your draft, and return it to you for revising.

Response Sheet G: Languages

Your name _____

The writer's name _____

Date _____

1. What is this essay about?

2. What do you like about the essay? Why?

3. What parts (if any) confuse you?

4. What questions do you have for the writer?

Tear out this sheet, and return it with the draft to the writer.

At Home

1. Read your draft, self-evaluation questions, Response Sheet G from your partner, and any comments from your teacher. Underline or mark anything that seems important to you.

2. On a separate sheet of paper, write briefly about how you plan to revise your draft. Consider the following questions:

   What do I want to add?

   What do I want to delete?

   What do I want to reorganize?

   What do I want to change (substitute)?

3. Reread your draft, making notes in the margin or on another sheet of paper about the revisions you would like to make.

4. Recopy your draft, incorporating the revisions you would like to make. Reread your revision, marking places where you are still not satisfied with what you wrote. You might want to revise again. When you are satisfied, make a neat copy of your latest version, write "Revision" at the top of the latest version, and clip everything together.

In Class

Exchange your drafts and revision with your partner. First read your partner's revision, making notes on another sheet of paper about what you liked and what you didn't understand. Write down any questions and suggestions you have about the revision to help your partner.

In Class

Return your partner's writing with your questions and suggestions, and read your partner's questions and suggestions about your own writing. Discuss any questions you have with your partner. Consider your partner's suggestions carefully, and decide whether to revise again. If you decide to revise, follow the same procedure you used to write the first revision. Clip all drafts, revisions, and comments together, and place this packet in your Writing Folder. Your teacher will collect your folder and comment on your revision.

At Home

Read the following excerpt from an article in the *San Francisco Chronicle* (January 2, 1987).

BATTLES OVER "ENGLISH-ONLY" ACROSS THE U.S.

Ann Scales minces no words when she discusses the prospect of English becoming the official language of her state.

"It is absolutely ridiculous and a complete insult," said Scales, a constitutional law expert who teaches at the University of New Mexico. "If your neighbors aren't named Martinez or Garcia, you don't live in New Mexico. This is the last place in America that legislation like that could ever work."

Bill Valentine also has a few words to say.

"For a long time, a lot of us have felt that some of the other cultures in our state would advance more quickly if they spoke English instead of their native tongue," said Valentine, the Republican leader in New Mexico's state Senate. "Bilingual education encourages these people to not learn the language of our society. We are very interested in pursuing English-only legislation."

These feelings are an outgrowth of California voters' approval last November of Proposition 63, which made English the official language of the state. It won a resounding 73 percent of the vote. Multilingual ballots, bilingual education and a variety of other government services can be challenged under the proposition, according to its supporters. . . .

In your Academic Journal, answer the following question about this excerpt:

What do you think about the efforts of some American legislators to make English the official language of the United States?

At Home

In your Academic Journal, write a letter to your teacher either explaining your opinion of the English-only movement or explaining what you learned in this chapter. Your teacher will collect your journal and respond to your letter.

At Home

Look at the words and phrases at the beginning of this chapter, and write them in your Academic Journal. What do they mean? Write the definition next to each word or phrase.

Summary

In this chapter you read and wrote about attitudes toward national and minority languages. In Chapter 6 you will write about childhood.

Children's Lives

In this chapter

—You will write about how children's lives have changed since you were a child and how you would raise your own children.

—You will edit one of the essays from this unit.

Words and Phrases to Watch For

Transformation   Proliferation

Vicissitudes   Epidemic

Upheavals   Child rearing

Childhood Then and Now

At Home

Answer the following prereading question in your Academic Journal:

How are the lives of children growing up today different from my life as a child?

In Class

1. Get into your writing group. Share your answers to the prereading question. Make a list of all the things your group members said about the lives of children today (Childhood Now) and another list about your lives as children (Childhood Then).

Childhood Now   *Childhood Then*

2. Share your lists with the other groups. With the class, try to discover the changes that have occurred in children's lives since you were a child. One student should make a list of these changes on the blackboard. Copy the list from the blackboard into your Academic Journal. Number the items on the list, and leave space between them.

At Home

Look at the class list of changes in children's lives. Under each item on the list, write an explanation of why you think this change occurred. An example from Giulia's journal follows:

They don't spend as much time with their family.

Kids today have money from their jobs or they get it from their parents, so they go with their friends to shopping and movies. They eat with their friends. Friends are their family now.

At Home

1. The following paragraph is adapted from *Children Without Childhood* by Marie Winn. Before reading the paragraph, consider what the book's title makes you think of. Spend five minutes writing about this in your journal.

2. Read the following paragraph. As you read, mark words, phrases, and sentences you think are interesting or important.

We have seen in an amazingly short span of time, a transformation of society's most fundamental attitudes toward children. Where parents once felt obliged to shelter their children from life's vicissitudes, today, great numbers of them have come to operate according to a new belief: that children must be exposed early to adult experience in order to survive in an increasingly uncontrollable world. The Age of Protection has ended. An Age of Preparation has set in. And children have suffered a loss. As they are integrated at a young age into the adult world, in every way their lives have become more difficult, more confusing—in short, more like adult lives. . . .

The Age of Protection did not end because of a deliberate decision to treat kids in a new way; it ended out of necessity. For children's lives are always a mirror of adult life. The great social upheavals of the late 1960's and early 1970's—the so-called sexual revolution, the drug epidemic, the women's movement, the breakdown of the conventional two-parent family, the spread of psychoanalytic thinking and the proliferation of television—each of these created changes in adult life that necessitated new ways of dealing with children. (pp. 64–65)

At Home

1. After reading the paragraph, answer the following questions in your Academic Journal:

   What changes in childhood does the author discuss?

   What reasons does she give for these changes?

   Is there anything she mentions that you don't understand?

2. Reread the paragraph. In your Academic Journal, take double-entry notes.

In Class

Get into your writing group. First, share your writing about the title *Children Without Childhood*. Next, share your double-entry notes. Take notes on the group discussion.

At Home

Review your answers to the prereading questions, your group and class lists about changes in childhood, your explanations of why these changes occurred, your double-entry notes, and your group discussion notes. Choose two or three topics from this writing that you would like to write more about.

In Class

Bring your list of topics to class. Meet with your group. Explain your choices to your group members. Let them help you decide which topic to write about.

Writing About What You Learned

At Home

1. At the top of one page of your Academic Journal, write the name of your topic. Then answer the following questions:

   What do I already know about this topic from my own experience, my observations, or my reading?

   What do I want to find out about this topic?

2. Read your answers to the questions. Write a two-part draft about (1) what you already know about your topic and (2) what you want to find out.

In Class

Bring your draft to class. Meet with a partner and share your drafts. Exchange drafts and fill out Response Sheet H. Return the draft and Response Sheet H to your partner. Make sure you both understand the responses.

Child Rearing

At Home

Complete the following sentences:

1. The role of a parent is

Response Sheet H:
Childhood Then and Now

Your name

The writer's name

Date

1. What is the topic of this draft?

2. What does the writer already know about this topic?

3. What does the writer want to find out about this topic?

4. What comments or suggestions do you have for the writer?

Tear out this response sheet, and return it with the draft to your partner.

2. The role of a child is

3. The relationship between a parent and a child is

In Class

Discuss your sentences with the whole class. Take discussion notes on the students' opinions about the role of a parent, the role of a child, and the relationship between a parent and a child.

At Home

In your Academic Journal, summarize the class discussion about parents and children. What are the differences of opinion about this topic? What are the points of agreement? Did anything you heard during the discussion surprise you?

At Home

The following paragraph is from a well-known guide for parents by Benjamin Spock. As you read the paragraph, mark words, phrases, and sentences you think are important.

It's basic human nature to tend to bring up your children about as you were brought up. . . . [I]f your upbringing was fairly strict in regard to obedience, manners, sex, truthfulness, it's natural, it's almost inevitable, that you will feel strongly underneath about such matters when raising your own children. You may have changed your theories because of something you've studied or read or heard, but when your child does something that would have been considered bad in your own childhood, you'll probably find yourself becoming more tense, or anxious, or angry than you imagined possible. (pp. 9–10)

Benjamin Spock, *Baby and Child Care*, 4th ed. (New York: Simon & Schuster, 1973). Copyright 1946, © 1957, 1968, 1976 by Benjamin Spock, M.D. Reprinted by permission of Pocket Books, a division of Simon & Schuster, Inc.

In your Academic Journal, answer the following questions about the paragraph:

1. What was difficult to understand about this paragraph?

2. What is your opinion of the author's ideas?

3. What questions do you want to ask during the class discussion?

4. How would you summarize this paragraph?

In Class

Bring your responses to class. Exchange journals with a partner. Write a response to your partner's entry. Explain what the entry made you think about. Return the journal to your partner, and read his or her response to your entry. Then, with your partner, think of one question or idea about child rearing you would like to discuss with the class.

In Class

Meet with the whole class. Raise your idea or question about child rearing. Listen to the responses and to the other questions and ideas. Take discussion notes.

At Home

Look over your notes from the discussion about child rearing. Summarize the discussion by answering the following question: What was the most interesting or important part of the discussion for you? Why? Spend fifteen minutes writing about this in your Academic Journal.

In Class

Share your summary of the class discussion with your group members. After sharing, make a list of possible topics related to child rearing you would like to write about. Giulia's list of possible topics follows:

rules for children — TV, candy, homework, bedtime
father's job in child rearing
good nutrition
what should I teach my children — reading?
English? money? manners?

At Home

Choose a topic from your list. Write a draft. Then answer the following questions:

Self-Evaluation Questions

1. What did I want to say about child rearing?

2. Was I successful?

3. What did I have problems with?

4. What parts of my draft need more work?

In Class

Exchange drafts with a partner. Read your partner's draft, and comment on it, using Response Sheet I. When your partner returns your draft and the response sheet, read the responses, and ask about anything you don't understand. Put the draft and response sheet in your Writing Folder. Your teacher will collect your folder, respond to your draft, and return your folder.

At Home

Choose one of the two drafts you wrote for this chapter to revise. Then do the following:

1. Read your draft. Then read the response sheet from your partner and any response from your teacher. Take notes about anything that seems important.

2. Reread your draft, making notes in the margins about the revisions you would like to make. If you plan to revise extensively, draft the changes on a new sheet of paper.

3. Recopy your draft, incorporating the changes you decided to make. Reread your revision, marking places where you are still not satisfied with what you have written. When you are satisfied with all the changes, make a neat copy of the final version. Clip everything together, and put the packet in your Writing Folder.

Editing a Draft

At Home

1. Look through your Writing Folder at all the drafts you have revised in this unit: Expectations and Surprises; Observations; Languages; Childhood Then and Now; and Child Rearing. Choose one of these

revisions to edit. Spend at least twenty minutes editing it. Don't erase anything. Just draw a line through the mistake and write the correction above. Mark (*) any sentences, phrases, or words you are unsure of.

2. In your editing log, make a list of the errors you found and corrected, and mark (*) the corrections you are unsure of.

In Class

Exchange edited revisions with a partner, and check your partner's revision. If you find a mistake your partner didn't find, underline it in pencil. When you have finished, talk to your partner about the mistakes you found in his or her revision. Help your partner with any corrections he or she is unsure of. Your teacher will help you and your partner with any problems.

At Home

Recopy the edited revision. Clip it to the notes, drafts, and revisions, and put this packet in your Writing Folder.

Unit Writing Folder Review

At Home

Reread all the work in your Writing Folder and your Academic Journal entries from this unit. Write a letter to your teacher about the work you have done. Tell your teacher what you have learned about culture shock, language and society, and childhood, and ask whatever questions you have. Your teacher will collect your Writing Folder and respond to your letter. Your teacher will also grade the edited text.

At Home

Look at the words and phrases at the beginning of this chapter, and write them in your Academic Journal. What do they mean? Write the definition next to each word or phrase.

Summary

In this chapter you wrote about changes in childhood and about child rearing. In Unit Three you will write about topics in the applied sciences.

Response Sheet I: Child Rearing

Your name _____

The writer's name _____

Date _____

1. What is the essay about?

2. What do you like about the essay? Why?

3. What parts (if any) confuse you?

4. What questions or comments do you have for the writer?

Tear out this sheet, and return it with the draft to the writer.

UNIT THREE

Writing About
Applied Sciences

In the next three chapters you will write about how
scientists work and how they try to apply scientific
knowledge to solve public problems. In Chapter 7,
you will write about how scientists work and about
the kinds of problems they face. In Chapter 8, you will
write about chemistry and ecology. In Chapter 9,
you will write about engineering and computer
technology.

CHAPTER 7

The Role of a Scientist

In this chapter

—You will study and write about the role of scientists in our world and the problems they face in doing their work.

—You will study and write about scientists' responsibilities to society.

Words and Phrases to Watch For

Hypothesis   Experiment   Phenomena

Data   Variables

How Scientists Work

At Home

Answer the following questions in the space provided.

1. What do scientists do?

2. What methods do they use?

3. What problems do they have?

4. What rewards do they receive?

In Class

In groups, share your responses to the questions with your group members. Choose someone in the group to be the recorder, and try to agree on a brief definition for the word *scientist*, using the group members' answers to the preceding questions. Have the recorder write the group's definition on a sheet of paper. Share your group's definition with your classmates, and discuss the other definitions. Ask questions about anything you do not understand.

In Class

In your Academic Journal, write a summary of the discussion about scientists. How do scientists work? What did you learn from the discussions? What questions do you still have?

At Home

Below is a list of steps scientists follow to find answers to their questions. Read the list and, as you read, mark places in the text that you think are interesting or important.

---

1. Ask a question (or identify a problem).
2. Make one or more hypotheses, or educated guesses, about what the answer (or solution) might be. This means using the process of induction: sorting through clues, hunches, and observations, then combining bits of information and logic to produce a general statement (the hypothesis).
3. Predict what the consequences might be if a hypothesis is valid. This process of reasoning from a general statement to predicting consequences is called deduction (and sometimes the "if-then" process).

4. Devise ways to test those deductions by making observations, developing models, or performing experiments.
5. Repeat the tests as often as necessary to determine whether results will be consistent and as predicted.
6. Report objectively on the tests and on conclusions drawn from them.
7. Examine alternative hypotheses in the same manner. (p. 19)

From *Biology: The Unity and Diversity of Life*, 4th ed., by Cecie Starr and Ralph Taggart. © 1987 by Wadsworth, Inc. Used by permission.

At Home

Reread the list of steps. In your Academic Journal, explain whether this list agrees or disagrees with your own description of how scientists work. Add to your explanation if you think it is necessary.

In Class

Get into your writing group and share your journal entries. Did any of your group members change their descriptions of what scientists do?

Formulating and Testing Hypotheses

At Home

In your Academic Journal, write a brief answer to the following questions:

—What is hypothesizing?
—How are hypotheses tested?

Read the following paragraphs (from Starr and Taggart, *Biology*). Mark any phrases or sentences you think are important.

How is it that scientists probe so skillfully into the monument of life and discover so much about its foundations? What is it about their manner of thinking that yields such precise results? Simply put, scientific inquiry routinely depends on systematic observation and test.

Observations can be made directly, through systems of vision, hearing, taste, olfaction, and touch. They can be made indirectly, through use of special equipment (such as a microscope) that extends the range of perception. With practice, we can become skilled at *making systematic observations*. This means focusing one or more senses on a particular object or event in the environment, and screening out the "background noise" of information that probably has no bearing on our focus.

Hypothesizing means putting together a tentative explanation to account for an observation. When a hypothesis is scientific, it is *testable* through experiments. Experiments are devised to test whether predictions that can be derived from the hypothesis are correct. Thus the hypothesis must be constructed so that it provides a framework for stating the results of an experiment. (p. 21)

Reread your answers to the preceding questions. Do you want to change or add to what you wrote in your Academic Journal?

At Home

After reading the paragraph about hypotheses, Raymond made a short list of hypotheses in his journal. He then wrote a brief explanation of the list. Read his list and the explanation that follows.

1. If I eat a lot of candy, I'll get cavities.
2. If I'm late for work a lot, I'll get fired.
3. If I do my home work, I'll get a good grade.
4. The sun will rise tomorrow at about 6:30 a.m.
5. Nuclear energy is cheap, clean, and safe.
6. Meat spoils when bacteria grows on it.

The first three hypotheses predict things that will happen to me, so they're personal hypotheses. I don't think the fourth one is really a hypothesis, because scientists know it already. I think the last two are more scientific, because they talk about things that happen in the world. So a hypothesis can have many different forms, and there can be personal ones as well as scientific ones. All five hypotheses can be tested.

Raymond then wrote an explanation of how he would test one of his hypotheses. His explanation follows:

I can look at two people. One eats lots of candy, and the other one doesn't. They can tell me how much candy they eat (how many pieces every day). Their dentists can tell me how many cavities they have. I think the person who eats more candy will have more cavities. But other things can influence this, for example how many times does he brush his teeth and does he have strong teeth.

At Home

In your Academic Journal, list some personal and scientific hypotheses of your own. Choose one personal hypothesis and one scientific hypothesis. Briefly describe how these two hypotheses could be tested.

In Class

Get into a small group, and share your journal entry with your group members. Choose one hypothesis and experiment to explain to the other groups. Use the blackboard, if necessary, to illustrate the experiment. After all the groups have presented their experiments, spend a few minutes writing in your journal about what was presented. Consider these questions:

—Which hypotheses will be easy to test? Which will be difficult?

—Which hypotheses interest you most? Why?

—Which experiments interest you most? Why?

At Home

Read the following paragraph about the scientist who discovered the vaccine for smallpox. As you read, mark places in the text that you think are interesting or important.

In about 1800, decades before the nature of disease-causing microorganisms was understood, an English country physician named Edward Jenner noted that milkmaids, whose hands were often scarred with cowpox, a common disease in cows, seldom had the much more serious human disease smallpox. Reasoning that the two diseases were related, Jenner proceeded to inoculate patients who had been exposed to smallpox with liquid taken from cowpox pustules; the patients failed to develop smallpox. Jenner coined the phrase "vaccination" (from the Latin *vacca*, meaning cow), and the term persists today. Jenner's success was based on the fact that cowpox and smallpox are caused by similar viruses, sharing common antigens. Antibodies to one are effective against the other. This was the beginning of modern vaccination for disease control. (p. 241)

From Mary E. Clark, *Contemporary Biology* (Philadelphia: W. B. Saunders, 1979).

At Home

In your Academic Journal, write a brief response to this paragraph. Consider the following questions:

—What was Jenner's hypothesis?

—What was his experiment?

—Do you approve of his experimental method? Why or why not?

In Class

Share your journal entries about the paragraph with your classmates. Was there any disagreement about Jenner's method?

In Class

Jacqueline imagined that she was the French doctor Daniel Zagury, who in 1986 vaccinated himself against the AIDS virus in order to test his vaccine.* This is what Jacqueline wrote in her draft:

Yesterday I did a very frightening thing, but it was something that I had to do. I have to test the AIDS vaccine on myself. How can I ask another one to do this? It is a big risk—my own life. But I think that this vaccine is good and that I will not get AIDS. I have made tests in the laboratory for 13 months. They make me think that the vaccine will work. Now I must wait to learn if my body can prevent the AIDS virus. I will tell the world what I have done, and may be other brave people will volunteer to help me. I hope and pray that I will succeed.

Discuss Jacqueline's draft with your classmates. Do you think it's realistic? How could Jacqueline change her draft to improve it?

At Home

Imagine you are a scientist and you have just decided to test your newest discovery on yourself or other people. Write a draft about your hopes and fears before testing your discovery and what results you anticipate. (Be sure to explain what your discovery is and what you hope it will do.) Imagine you will eventually publish this as a newspaper article. When you have finished writing this draft, answer the following questions on an extra sheet of paper, and attach this page to your draft.

Self-Evaluation Questions

1. What was I trying to say in this draft?

2. Am I happy with what I wrote?

3. What did I have problems with?

4. What parts of my draft need more work?

---

* See article "Their Lives on the Line" in the Appendix, p. 163.

Share your draft with a partner, and have your partner fill out Response Sheet J. Read the response sheet, and ask your partner to explain anything you didn't understand. Listen to your partner's draft, and fill out Response Sheet J for your partner. Put your draft, self-evaluation, and response sheet in your Writing Folder. Your teacher will collect your folder and respond to your draft.

Solving Public Problems

At Home

In your Academic Journal, list different public problems scientists have tried to solve in the past or are trying to solve now. (The vaccines for smallpox and AIDS are two examples of public problems scientists have worked to solve.) Choose two problems from your list and write everything you know about them. As you are writing, consider the following questions:

—Is this a current problem or one that was solved in the past?

—How many people are affected by this problem?

—What was/is needed to solve the problem?

—How might the solution create new problems?

—For a current problem, do you think a solution is possible?

—For a past problem, do you think the solution was the best one?

In Class

Share your Academic Journal entry about the two problems with your writing group. Take notes on the responses you get from your group. After all the group members have had a chance to share their entries, decide which problem you want to write about. Explain your choice in your Academic Journal.

At Home

Danny shared his Academic Journal entry with his writing group, and together they brainstormed ways he could expand his journal entry into a draft. Read his journal entry and his notes on the group's responses to it.

Response Sheet J:
Self-Experimentation Draft

Your name _____

The writer's name _____

Date _____

1. What is the writer's newest discovery, and what is it supposed to do?

2. What are the writer's hopes and fears about the experiment?

3. What do you like about this draft? Why?

4. What parts (if any) confuse you?

5. What questions do you have for the writer?

Tear out this sheet, and return it with the draft to the writer.

Two problems: population explosion in my country, and tuberculosis. I know very much about #1, but no very much about #2. But I'm interesting in it. For population explotion, my goverment tries every thing to help people to have less children. Laws, education, "peer pressure," but not success. People like to have many children. I think education is best solution, and I think birth control should be free. Scientists can help, because they can do experiments to find best birth control and then tell us.

Many years ago tuberculosis was a big problem every where, but now it isn't. Scientists found a cure for it. I think this cure help make the population explosion because less people died. My grandmother's friend had it, and I asked her to tell me about him. She doesn't like to talk about it because he was too sick. She doesn't like to remember. He's dead now.

Here are Danny's notes on the responses he received:

Nadia, Carlos, and Paul are in my group.
Nadia doesn't like to read about TB. Population explosion is interesting. Everyone wants to solve this problem. I should write about that. What do I think about abortions?
What laws in my country about population explosion?
What does "peer pressure" mean?
Paul thinks I will be easier to write about #1, because I know about it. #2 is too difficult. I don't know enough.

At Home

Danny used his group's comments to help him write a draft about the population explosion in his country. Read his draft. How did Danny use his group members' responses to write his draft?

Population Explosion in China Today

Everyone know that in China today is big population explosion. We are more than 1 billion people, and there are too many problems for this. We have too little food, and schools are too crowded with children. The big cities are very difficult to find apartments for everyone. Every family in China want many children, because children mean happiness to Chinese parent.

Chinese government made new laws for this. For example, parents can to have only two children. This is difficult for farmers, because they need many children to help them. But I think that the farmers can get other people to come and help them. These people can be "adopted children" for them. Also I think birth control should be free. Farmers are poor and cannot pay for this.

It is easier to control population in the cities, because the radio and the television can tell people what to do. Also big signs in the cities tell people "Small families are better". Everyday a parent is reading the signs and listening the programs on tv and radio. He or she will think carefully about how many children does he want.

Education on tv, radio, and signs will help Chinese people to learn about population explosion and solutions. Chinese scientists can experiment to find best birth control methods. If Chinese people work together and try hard, we will success.

At Home

Use your group's comments to help you write a draft about the public problem you chose from the list in your Academic Journal. When you have finished writing this draft, answer the following questions on an extra sheet of paper, and attach this page to your draft.

Self-Evaluation Questions

1. What was I trying to say in this draft?

2. Am I happy with what I wrote?

3. What did I have problems with?

4. What parts of my draft need more work?

In Class

Share your draft with a partner. Have your partner fill out Response Sheet K. Read the response sheet, and ask your partner to explain anything you didn't understand. Listen to your partner's draft, and fill out Response Sheet K. Put your draft and response sheet in your Writing Folder. Your teacher will collect your folder and respond to your draft.

Response Sheet K:
The Scientific Problem

Your name

The writer's name

Date

1. What problem is this essay about?

2. What do you like about this essay? Why?

3. What parts (if any) confuse you?

4. What questions do you have for the writer?

Tear out this sheet, and return it with the draft to the writer.

At Home

Reread the two drafts you wrote in this chapter: the one about self-experimentation and the one about a public problem. Reread Response Sheets J and K and your answers to the self-evaluation questions, and read your teacher's comments. Decide which of these two drafts you would like to revise, and follow the same procedure that you used with other drafts.

In Class

In your Academic Journal, write a letter to your teacher about what you learned from reading about the responsibilities and problems scientists face and from writing about these responsibilities and problems. Your teacher will collect your Academic Journal and respond to your letter.

At Home

Look at the words and phrases at the beginning of this chapter, and write them in your Academic Journal. What do they mean? Write the definition next to each word or phrase.

Summary

In this chapter you read and wrote about the responsibilities and problems scientists face when doing their work. In Chapter 8 you will read and write about specific issues in the field of chemistry.

CHAPTER 8

Chemistry

In this chapter

—You will study and write about chemistry.

—You will design and conduct an observation project.

—You will write a report of your project.

Words and Phrases to Watch For

Chemicals   Elements

Pollution   Conduct

What Is Chemistry?

At Home

In your Academic Journal, spend about fifteen minutes writing about the topic "Chemistry." Summarize what you know, and write questions you have about this topic.

In Class

Share your journal entry with your classmates. Have a recorder write the students' questions on the blackboard. In your Academic Journal, write any questions that seem interesting to you.

In Class

Read the following passage on the chemical elements, marking the words or phrases you think are important. In your Academic Journal, draw a line down the middle of a page, and take double-entry notes on the passage.

Everything in the world is made up of chemical elements. Most of us know that water is made up of hydrogen and oxygen elements that have combined in a specific way: two bits of hydrogen with one bit of oxygen. Another word for each of these bits is "atom." When atoms of different elements combine, the combination is called a molecule. Thus, two hydrogen atoms combined with one oxygen atom make a molecule of water, abbreviated as H_2O by chemists.

Carbon is an element found almost everywhere. Every living (organic) thing contains carbon elements, as well as some non-living (inorganic) things. Carbon combines easily with oxygen to form carbon monoxide (CO) and carbon dioxide (CO_2); and various combinations of carbon, hydrogen, and oxygen make up the different sugars that we eat (sucrose, lactose, and fructose, for example).

Each chemical element is made up of a nucleus and electrons. The nucleus is the center of the atom, and the electrons circle the nucleus, just as satellites circle the earth. The nucleus itself is made up of protons and neutrons, and the number of protons in an atom usually equals the number of electrons. The nucleus is positively charged and the electrons are negatively charged, thus balancing each other out. But atoms become unstable if they lose electrons, making them more likely to combine with other atoms to form molecules.

In Class

Review the questions written on the blackboard about chemistry, and try to answer some of the questions that were recorded. Does the preceding passage help you answer any of the questions? When you are finished, share your answers with your classmates.

At Home

In your Academic Journal, list areas where you think knowledge of chemistry is important or can help solve problems. Circle two areas on your list that seem interesting to you. Write briefly about why these two areas interest you.

At Home

After Carlos made his list, he circled "air pollution" and "not enough food—famine." He then wrote:

These are problems in everywhere of the world. Air pollution makes people and animals to get sick. No enough food also big problem. I think chemists can find solutions. I don't know how.

Finally, Carlos listed some questions he had about these two problems:

1. What causes air pollution? What are bad chemicals in the air? Do these chemicals hurt plants? If I see sick or dying plants, what makes them to get sick? Air pollution?

2. Why is there not enough food in the world? How we can grow more? Can chemicals help? How chemicals can help?

At Home

Look back at the two items you circled on your list. Spend about ten minutes listing all the questions you have about these two items.

In Class

In a small group, share your list and questions about areas where knowledge of chemistry can be important or helpful. (This group will be your research group.)

1. Read your list and questions aloud, and explain them to your group members. Have them help you choose one to continue working on.

2. Have your group members help you list more questions for the area you chose.

3. Take notes on your group members' comments.

4. Repeat this process for each group member.

Designing an Observation Project

Being able to observe carefully is important for chemists, who must detect small changes during their experiments. We won't ask you to conduct chemical experiments, but we will ask you to observe something carefully and try to explain what you have observed.

At Home

After sharing his questions with his small group, Carlos reread his notes and began thinking about how he could find answers to his questions. He wrote the following:

I want to do pollution because is too hard to do famine. I live in a city with too much pollution so I can look around this city and see things. Even I can observe the streets, how many cars there are. On my street, the trees are sick, and there are too many traffics. I can count the traffics on my street and compare to another street that has healthy trees.

Carlos then made some brief notes about the design of his observation project:

1. Find a street with health trees.
   Describe. What trees look like.

2. Observe traffics.
   How many cars, trucks, buses.
   People walking.
   Write down time of day.

3. Do same with my street.

4. Observe at different times.

In Class

Reread the questions and notes you made about areas where knowledge of chemistry can be helpful. In your Academic Journal, write for ten minutes about the questions on your list. How can you find answers to some of them? Is there something you can observe to help you answer the questions? Share your writing with your research group, and help each other design observation projects that will help you answer your questions.

At Home

In your Academic Journal, write briefly about your observation project. Where do you plan to go? How much time do you need for the observation? What do you need to watch for? What do you hope to learn?

Conducting an Observation Project

At Home

Carlos conducted his observation project and took careful notes. Part of his notes, in double-entry form, follow. Note that he wrote the observation notes in the left-hand column and his responses in the right-hand column.

May 13, Wed
8:17–8:27 a.m.
neighborhood A
100+ cars go south, 27 go north;
3 buses south, 1 bus north;
no trucks; 5 parked cars leave,
no cars park

Rush hour, more people commute downtown than uptown; 17 cars (16 down & 1 up) had exhaust that I can see; all buses had some exhaust—is this mean that these buses & cars pollute more than cars without some exhaust?

May 15, Fri
12:15–12:25 p.m.
neighborhood A
3 cars south, 5 north; 1 bus
south, 1 bus north; no trucks;
1 car parks

is very quiet now; most people are at work; is a lot of people out walking, with dogs or sons. Is the time for families to be outside.

May 18, Mon
5:20–5:30
neighborhood B
1 truck makes a delivery; 20
cars go north, 3 cars go south;
no buses or other trucks;
10 cars park

Is rush hour now, but here isn't a major road; a lot of the cars were going slowly (looking for parking spaces?). I think these people drive into this neighborhood because they live in it. In neighborhood A, most of the people probably don't live in it.

Summary: Is a lot more traffic in neighborhood A, because is a big road. The trees that are on a small road look healthier than the trees on the big road. So I think that the number of cars and buses affects the trees. Fewer cars means healthier trees.

Discuss Carlos's notes with your classmates. What do you notice about how he wrote them? Do you think Carlos was beginning to find answers to his questions about pollution? Why or why not?

At Home

Conduct your observation, being sure to take careful notes. You might want to draw a line down the middle of several pages and keep your notes on the left-hand side and write comments on the right-hand side (like double-entry notes). When you have finished, spend a few minutes writing a summary of your thoughts about your observation.

Writing an Observation Report

At Home

Carlos met again with his research group and shared his notes with his group members. They asked him questions and discussed his observations. Carlos wrote the following about the meeting with his research group:

My group didn't have too much questions. They want to know why did I observe at morning, noon, and evening. They also want to know more about neighborhood A and B. I told them that A is busy, and has some stores, and B is more homes and apartments. Nadia asked me if I saw parking lots. Is no parking lots in A or B. They agree with me that cars and buses are bad for trees. We disagreed which is worse, cars or buses. Bus makes more pollution than car, but is more cars than buses.

In Class

Meet with your research group, and share your observation notes with each other.

1. Ask questions about anything that is unclear to you in your group members' notes, and help your group members summarize what they saw.

2. Write briefly in your journal about your group's response to your observation notes. What questions did they have? What suggestions did they make?

At Home

Carlos reread everything in his Academic Journal about his observation project (his initial questions and ideas, his observation notes, and his research group's various responses to his ideas). Using his notes, he wrote a draft of his observation report. Read his draft below, marking parts that confuse you and parts that interest you.

I observed two neighborhoods to see how air pollution can be hurting trees. Neighborhood A is a busy neighborhood. It has stores and businesses, and is a lot of traffic there. In the morning 100 cars drove on the street in only 10 minutes. That's mean 10 cars every minute. Rush hour is 7:30–9:00, or 90 minutes, so that's mean 900 cars on that street every morning. Is also buses and trucks, but no as many.

Neighborhood B is no as busy. Is mostly homes and one apartment building. In the morning only 23 cars drove on this street in 10 minutes, so only 200 cars during rush hours, I didn't see no buses or trucks. So neighborhood A has more traffics than neighborhood B.

In A the trees are very bad. Some with brown leaves. Most trees have only little leaves. A businessman in his office said me that "These trees are 10 years old, but they look like 5 years old. They don't grow well on this street." I think he means the pollution hurts them.

In B the trees are good, they look like healthy. They are tall, and they have too many leaves.

I think the more cars in A have hurt the trees there. We should find a way to stop the pollution and make these trees get healthy.

In Class

Discuss Carlos's draft with your classmates.

1. How did Carlos use his observation notes and group members' questions to write his draft?

2. What do you like about Carlos's draft? What questions do you have about it?

3. What can Carlos change to improve his draft?

At Home

Reread everything in your Academic Journal about your observation project (your initial questions and ideas, observation notes, and research group's various responses to your ideas). Using your notes, write a draft of your observation report. When you have finished writing this draft, answer the following questions on an extra sheet of paper, and attach this page to your draft.

Self-Evaluation Questions

1. What was I trying to say in this draft?

2. Am I happy with what I wrote?

3. What did I have problems with?

4. What parts of my draft need more work?

In Class

Share your draft with one of the members from your research group. Have your partner fill out Response Sheet L. Read the response sheet, and ask your partner to explain anything you didn't understand. Listen to your partner's draft, and fill out Response Sheet L. Put your draft and response sheet in your Writing Folder. Your teacher will collect your folder and respond to your draft.

At Home

Revise the draft of your observation report, following the procedure you used with other revisions. When you have finished revising, place the draft and revision in your Writing Folder.

In Class

In your Academic Journal, write a letter to your teacher about what you learned from reading about chemistry and from writing an observation report. Your teacher will collect your Academic Journal and respond to your letter.

At Home

Look at the words and phrases at the beginning of this chapter, and write them in your Academic Journal. What do they mean? Write the definition next to each word or phrase.

Summary

In this chapter you read about chemistry, you designed an observation project to help you answer questions you had, and you wrote and revised an observation report. In Chapter 9 you will read about technological sciences, and you will write a technological report.

Response Sheet L: Observation Report

Your name

The writer's name

Date

1. What was the writer observing?

2. What did the writer learn from this observation?

3. What do you like about this draft? Why?

4. What parts (if any) confuse you?

5. What questions do you have for the writer?

Tear out this sheet, and return it with the draft to the writer.

CHAPTER 9

Engineering and Computer Technology

In this chapter

—You will study and write about engineering and computer technology.

—You will write technological reports analyzing a structure and explaining a process.

Words and Phrases to Watch For

Analysis	Technology
Process	Computers
Structure	Engineers

What Are Technological Sciences?

In Class

In a small group, choose a recorder to keep notes, and discuss the following questions:

1. What do engineers do? How do they help society?

2. What do computer scientists do? How do they help society?

3. What are some other technological sciences?

4. How do the various technological sciences affect each other?

Report your group's answers to the whole class. Choose a class recorder to write brief notes of the discussion on the blackboard. Copy these notes into your Academic Journal.

At Home

Read the following paragraph from a book about engineering.

New York City's Pan Am Building, rising 808 feet from the taxi-laden street to the helicopter-landing pad on its roof, is a major accomplishment in every sense. It is more than 10 times taller than the original height of the Sumerian ziggurat at Ur and encloses five times more space than the cathedral of Notre Dame in Paris. Its statistics are dazzling: it contains 60 acres of offices and 17,000 permanent workers—plus the 250,000 or so people who visit or pass through the building every day. The 59 floors are served by 18 moving stair-ways and 65 elevators, some of which shoot upward at 25 feet a second. The building uses 2,000 gallons of water every minute and as much electricity and telephone service as 10,000 homes. To allow for telephone demand, in fact, the New York Telephone Company had to install an $11-million, city-sized centralized exchange—the first ever devised for one building—with 1,000 tons of equipment on the 21st and part of the 20th floors. (p. 101)

From C. C. Furnas, Joe McCarthy, and the Editors of *Life, The Engineer.* © 1971 Time-Life Books, Inc. Used by permission.

In your Academic Journal, answer the following questions about the paragraph:

1. What was difficult to understand about this paragraph?

2. What is your opinion about the writer's ideas?

3. What questions do you want to ask during the class discussion?

4. How would you summarize this paragraph (in one or two sentences)?

In Class

In a small group, discuss your answers to the questions. Then reread the discussion notes in your Academic Journal. Do you want to add to the definition of what engineers do and how they help society? What would you like to add?

At Home

Reread your notes from the class discussion of engineering.

1. Spend a few minutes brainstorming a list of items you see around you that might have been designed by engineers. Your list might begin:

   Mechanical pencil

   Electric coffee pot

   Pencil sharpener

   What other items can you add to this list?

2. Look over your list, and choose two or three items you are curious about. Write in your Academic Journal about each of these items. Consider the following questions:

   What does it look like?

   What do people use it for?

   How has it helped people?

   How do you think it works?

In Class

Share your journal entry with a partner. What does your partner know about the items you described in your entry? Take notes on any interesting comments your partner makes. Have your partner help you choose one of the items to analyze carefully and write about. Then discuss your partner's journal entry.

Writing an Analysis of a Structure

In Class

Nadia chose "paperclip" from her list of items. In her journal, she had written the following entry about paperclips:

> It is some kind of metal, very thin, with three turns in it. I can bend it, so the metal is not strong. People use it to put together papers, and it's very helpful for this. People always want paperclips. Is not easy to describe how it works. One half of the clip is on top and another half is on the bottom, the two halves are tight together, so they hold the paper.

Nadia also wrote down the following comments from her partner:

He said there are plastic paperclips, and also different shapes. He agreed with me to say I can't describe how it works.

Nadia then wrote the following analysis of a paperclip:

Paperclips are everywhere. People use them in school, in business, in home, everywhere. The paperclips help the people hold their papers together. If people didn't have a paperclip, they could lose their papers.

A paperclip is metal or plastic, it is different shapes. Usually you see a thin, round piece of metal, about 4 inches long, with three turns, so the clip is only about 1 inch long.

A paperclip will hold many papers together. One turn of the paperclip is inside another one, so you can easy to put it on the papers. One half of the clip is on top and another half is on the bottom, the two halves are tight together, so they hold the paper.

How did Nadia use her notes and her partner's comments to write her analysis?

At Home

Reread your journal entry about the items that might have been designed by engineers, and reread the notes you wrote about your partner's comments. Write a draft about the structure of one item on your list. You can use the questions on p. 113 to help you.

When you have finished writing this draft, answer the following questions on an extra sheet of paper, and attach this page to your draft.

Self-Evaluation Questions

1. What was I trying to say in this draft?

2. Am I happy with what I wrote?

3. What did I have problems with?

4. What parts of my draft need more work?

In Class

Share your draft with a partner. Have your partner fill out Response Sheet M. Read the response sheet, and ask your partner to explain anything you didn't understand. Listen to your partner's draft, and fill out Response Sheet M for your partner. Put your draft, self-evaluation, and response

Response Sheet M: Analyzing a Structure

Your name

The writer's name

Date

1. What structure is the writer analyzing?

2. What are the different parts of the structure?

3. What do you like about this draft? Why?

4. What parts (if any) confuse you?

5. What questions do you have for the writer?

Tear out this sheet, and return it with the draft to the writer.

sheet in your Writing Folder. Your teacher will collect your folder and respond to your draft.

What Is Computer Technology?

In Class

Read the following paragraphs from a book about computer science. As you read, mark phrases or sentences that seem important to you. After you finish reading, try to list other examples of computer simulations. Write double-entry notes about the paragraphs in your Academic Journal.

What makes simulation different from other computer applications? Computer simulation is exciting because it deals with complex problems in economics, nature, society, and human life. It is one of the most valuable types of computer applications in that it can often be accomplished *only* by computer. . . .

A *simulation* is an approximation of the way an environment will operate under varying conditions. . . . The approximation is called a *model* of the environment being studied. . . .

Computer simulation computationally evaluates models of real or hypothetical environments as they might vary, generally over time. It is often used when the number of possibilities or combinations of possibilities that might occur that could affect something is very large. Through computer simulation all possible combinations are tested and individual outcomes are presented. . . .

[For example,] computer simulation is used to *design and engineer structures and transport modes*—buildings, automobiles, highways, aircraft and spacecraft, nuclear reactors, and a myriad of other items. . . . A superhighway, for example, is simulated over many different possible routes to evaluate and compare certain costs (such as those involved with the amount of earth that has to be moved) with the costs of the right-of-way and other considerations. (pp. 233–235)

From *The Computer Chronicles*, by H. D. Lechner. © 1984 by Wadsworth, Inc. Used by permission.

In Class

In a small group, share your list of computer simulation examples. As a group, choose one to discuss in detail. Try to list the components of the simulation model. For example, the components of the superhighway model would include terrain, weather, cost and availability of various materials, traffic volume, and so on. Share your model and list of components with your classmates.

Writing a Description of a Process

Engineers and computer scientists need to be able to break a process down into its various steps in order to analyze those steps. We cannot expect you to be able to analyze complicated technological processes, so we will ask you to analyze a process you are familiar with.

At Home

Ronak made the following list in his Academic Journal of activities that involve a number of steps:

> do homework, make dinner, drive a car, solve an algebra problem, grow grain, take a photograph, write a computer program

Ronak then wrote the following notes about growing grain:

> Trees and seeds, pumps and canals flow water, machines separate plant from stem, people separate grain from plant sunlight — take skin off, weighted (get etc.), grain market etc.

At Home

In your Academic Journal, list activities that involve a number of steps. These can be simple or complex activities. From your list, choose two or three activities that interest you most, and write briefly about the steps involved in each of them.

In Class

In a small group, share your journal entry about the two or three activities. Ask your group members if they have any questions about the steps involved, and take notes on your group members' comments.

In Class

Read Ronak's draft about the process of growing grain. What questions do you have about Ronak's draft, and what suggestions do you have for revising it? Share your questions and suggestions with your classmates.

One Part of Village Life

The people in the villages all the day work in the farm or the fields do the plowing and cultivate the fields. They plants the trees and put the seeds in the field. Then with the help of the turbine pumps and the canals or the ditches they flow water through the fields and as a result the crop grows more and more.

At the time of harvesting members of the whole family get together and they work hard for the whole day in the field with their grown crop. They get the machines and separate the plant from the stem and tie it together in a bundle then put in a cart and bring under the tree and start separating the grain from the plant they bought.

The grain which is separated from the plant is then put down in the sunlight and after two or three days they start taking the skin from the seeds. Further the separated seeds are then pour down in the plastic bags and then they are weighed in the government office.

From the government office they are loaded in the trucks and send down to the city. Thus the grain from the field is in the city with in two weeks. Then they are in grain market and the price in the grain market is maintained by the stock holders. The new price of the grain is made. When this grain is put down on the shelf of the market the people buy the grain.

When all the grain is sold out the money is collected by the government and is send down too the villagers back. The money come back and the villager becomes happy and they use this money for the new and the better grain for the next year.

At Home

Reread your notes in your Academic Journal about the activities and steps involved in doing them, as well as the notes on your group members' comments. Choose one of the activities and, using your notes, write a draft describing the steps involved. When you have finished writing this draft, answer the following questions on an extra sheet of paper, and attach this page to your draft.

Self-Evaluation Questions

1. What was I trying to say in this draft?

2. Am I happy with what I wrote?

3. What did I have problems with?

4. What parts of my draft need more work?

In Class

Share your draft with a partner, and have your partner fill out Response Sheet N. Read the response sheet, and ask your partner to explain anything you didn't understand. Listen to your partner's draft, and fill out Response Sheet N. Put your draft, self-evaluation questions, and response sheet in your Writing Folder. Your teacher will collect your folder and respond to your draft.

At Home

Revise the two drafts you wrote for this chapter (analyzing a structure and describing a process), following the procedure you used for other revisions.

At Home

Use the following procedures to edit three of the most recent revisions in your Writing Folder.

1. Choose one of the revisions in your Writing Folder. Spend at least twenty minutes editing it. Don't erase anything. Just draw a line through the mistake and write the correction above. Mark (*) any sentences, phrases, or words you are unsure of.

2. In your editing log, make a list of the errors you found and corrected, and mark (*) the corrections you are unsure of.

3. Repeat steps one and two for your other revisions.

In Class

Exchange one of your edited revisions with a partner, and check your partner's revision. If you find a mistake your partner didn't find, underline it in pencil. When you have finished, talk to your partner about the mistakes you found in his or her revision. Help your partner with any corrections he or she is unsure of. Your teacher will help you and your partner with any problems.

Response Sheet N: Describing a Process

Your name _____

The writer's name _____

Date _____

1. What process is the writer describing?

2. What do you like about this draft? Why?

3. What parts (if any) confuse you?

4. What questions do you have for the writer?

Tear out this sheet, and return it with the draft to the writer.

At Home

Make a clean copy of your edited revision, including any corrections your partner made. Clip this copy together with all the notes and drafts, and put it in your Writing Folder. Your teacher will collect your Writing Folder to comment on your work.

Unit Writing Folder Review

At Home

Reread the work in your Writing Folder that you did for this unit as well as your Academic Journal entries. Write a letter to your teacher about the work you have done. Tell what you have learned about writing about natural and applied sciences, and ask whatever questions you have. Choose one of your edited texts for your teacher to grade. Your teacher will collect your Writing Folder and respond to your letter, and he or she will also grade the text you chose.

At Home

Look at the words and phrases at the beginning of this chapter, and write them in your Academic Journal. What do they mean? Write the definition next to each word or phrase.

Summary

In this chapter you read about engineering and computer technology, and you wrote reports analyzing a structure and describing a process. In Unit Four you will write about art and poetry and put together a class magazine.

UNIT FOUR

Writing About Humanities

In this unit you will write about the humanities: visual arts and poetry. You will respond to short texts and discuss and revise your written responses. The focus of this unit is the uniqueness of each student's response. You will write about how and why the students' written responses to art and texts differ.

CHAPTER 10

Visual Arts

In this chapter

—You will respond in writing to photographs and drawings.

—You will share your responses with other students to discover the different ways art affects people.

Words and Phrases to Watch For

Uniqueness   Speculate

Visual arts   Caption

Archives

Responding to Photographs

At Home

Answer the following questions. Write in the spaces below each question.

1. What experience(s) have you had looking at works of art?

2. How do you feel when someone asks you to explain or describe a work of art?

In Class

Share and discuss your answers to the preceding questions with your classmates.

At Home

In the following passage, Jean Mohr, a photographer for the United Nations, tells about a time he asked different people to explain what they saw in some of his photographs.

I took a number of photographs from my archives and I went out to look for those who would explain them. Of the ten people I asked, only one refused. He was an old gardener and he said it was too much like a television guessing-game.

All the others agreed to describe what came into their minds when presented with the photo I was showing them. I said nothing myself, simply noting what was said. The choice of people was largely a matter of chance. Some were acquaintances, others I was seeing for the first time. (p. 42)

From John Berger and Jean Mohr, *Another Way of Telling* (New York: Pantheon, 1982).

In Figure 10.1 on p. 128 you will see a photograph that was shown to some students and teachers. Before reading their responses, write in your Academic Journal about what comes to mind when you look at it. What do you see? What does it make you think of?

Now read what the students and teachers said about this photograph. After the three responses, you can read the photographer's explanation of where the photograph was taken and what was happening.

Barry Antokoletz, ESL teacher: In this photograph is conveyed basically a feeling of desperate need on the part of the black citizen—desperate because this adult has had to stoop now to appealing to children. He wants something from the white establishment and has been rejected. Perhaps innocent children will give him the basics of what he needs, free of the sophisticated, guileful political considerations of their elders.

Figure 10.1

Yves Belancourt, George Luces, Rui Zhang, Hui Juan Liang, ESL students: In our opinion, the main idea of this photo shows that there is a segregation between the white people and the black people. You see the two little white girls try to walk away from the black man. But the black man really likes the two little girls. He tries to get close to the girls and talks to them. But the girls do not care about the man; just walk away.

Paula Sloan, ESL teacher: This photograph is formally beautiful. The motion of the figures and the angle of the wheel cause an interesting tension. Questions are also raised as to what the wheel belongs to, what the relationship is among the people, and where the photo was taken. The presence of the black man in non-Western dress causes me to place the photograph in a very different context than I would if he were not there. All photographs are poignant in that they freeze a moment. This one is especially so because it is mysterious.

Photographer: In 1960 I was visiting Zanzibar with my wife and three daughters. After checking into our hotel, we went for a walk. As we passed by a rickshaw (carriage), the driver asked my youngest daughters if they wanted to go for a ride.

Spend ten minutes writing in your Academic Journal about the differences in the responses (including your own) to the photograph. What did each of the people see in the photograph? What surprised or interested you in their reactions? What were the differences in their reactions? How are the responses different from the photographer's explanation of what was happening?

In Class

Share your own written response to the photograph with your group members. What differences did you find in the responses of your group members?

At Home

Choose a photograph you have of your family, friends, or a place you visited or lived in. In your Academic Journal, spend fifteen minutes writing an explanation of this photograph to someone who does not know the people or place. Tell where, when, and why the photograph was taken.

In Class

Choose three people in your class who are not in your group. Show your photograph to these three students, and ask each of them to tell you what they see. Write down their responses. If you have a tape recorder, you can record the responses and later transcribe them. Before each response, write some information about the person you interviewed (age, sex, native country, field of study).

Writing a Draft About the Photograph

At Home

Reread the three responses to your photograph. Think about the differences and similarities. Speculate about why they are different or similar. Next, write a draft about your photograph and the responses of the three students you interviewed. Begin with the three responses, including some information about each student. Add the explanation you wrote in your Academic Journal about the photograph. Finally, write about how the three responses were different, and explain your reaction to the responses.

In Class

Exchange drafts with a partner. Read your partner's draft, and comment on it using Response Sheet O. When your partner returns your draft with the response sheet, read it carefully and ask about any comments you do not understand. Then clip everything together, and put it in your Writing Folder. Your teacher will collect your folder, respond to your draft, and return it to you for revising.

At Home

Revise the draft of the photograph paper, following the procedure you used for other revisions. When you have finished revising, place the draft and revisions in your Writing Folder.

In Class

Study the photograph in Figure 10.2. Imagine that you must interview the woman in the photograph to learn about her life. With the other class members, write ten interview questions to ask the woman. Write these questions in the space provided on p. 133. Your questions should address the woman in the photograph directly, for example, "Where were you born?"

Figure 10.2

Response Sheet O: Photograph

Your name

The writer's name

Date

1. What was the writer's explanation of the photograph?

2. What were the three responses to the photograph?

3. What differences did the writer notice in the responses?

4. What was the writer's reaction to the three responses?

Tear out this sheet, and return it with the draft to the writer.

Class Questions

1.

2.

3.

4.

5.

6.

7.

8.

9.

10.

1. Meet with a partner. One partner will act as the woman in the photograph; the other will act as the interviewer. The interviewer will use the class questions to interview the student acting as the woman in the photograph about her life. The interviewer will take notes to record the answers. Save the interview notes for a class discussion.

2. Using the interview notes, you and your partner will write a few paragraphs telling about the woman's life. Imagine that these paragraphs will be used as a caption for the photograph to tell about the woman's life. The caption will be written in the woman's own voice (first person).

In Class

You and your partner will share your caption with the rest of the class. Explain how you used the notes to write the caption. Listen to the other captions and explanations of how the partners used their notes. Discuss the differences in your captions and explanations.

At Home

In your Academic Journal, write about what you learned from listening to your classmates' captions and explanations of the process of writing them.

Responding to Drawings

In Class

Figure 10.3 shows a drawing by Swiss artist Paul Klee (1879–1940). Find a partner in the class, and discuss the drawing with this person. Tell your partner what you imagine the figures in the drawing are doing and who they are.

Writing a Story About the Drawing

At Home

Write a story about the figures in the drawing. Give them names. Tell where, when, and how they live. Explain what is happening in the picture. Also explain the relationship between the picture and your story. In other

Figure 10.3

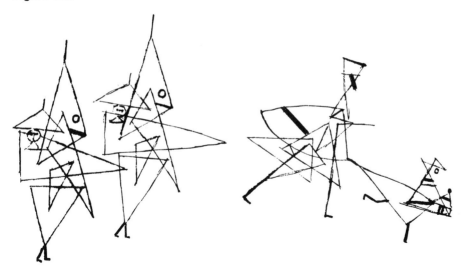

Reprinted by permission of Leon Amiel Publishing.

words, tell how your story fits this drawing: Why do you believe your story is a good one for this drawing?

In Class

Share your story with your group members. What were the similarities and differences in your stories? Did all of the stories seem to fit well with the drawing? Why or why not?

At Home

The same questions you answered at the beginning of the chapter follow. Write in the spaces below the questions.

1. What experience(s) have you had looking at works of art?

2. How do you feel when someone asks you to explain or describe a work of art?

Compare the answers you wrote at the beginning of the chapter with the answers you just wrote. Then write a letter to your teacher about what you learned from working on this chapter. Put this letter in your Writing Folder.

At Home

Look at the words and phrases at the beginning of this chapter, and write them in your Academic Journal. What do they mean? Write the definition next to each word or phrase.

Summary

In this chapter you responded to two photographs and a drawing, and you wrote about responding to visual art. In Chapter 11 you will read and write about poems.

Poetry

In this chapter

—You will respond to and write poems. Reading and writing poems in English is a way to learn more about the sound and structure of the language.

—You will share your responses and your poems to discover each student's unique ways of using language and responding.

Words and Phrases to Watch For

Unique	Stanza
Distinctive	Metaphor
Images	Abstract concept

Translating a Poem

At Home

Answer the following questions in your Academic Journal.

1. What experience do you have reading poetry in your native language? In English?

2. What experience do you have writing poems in your native language? In English?

3. Do you like poetry? Why or why not?

In Class

Get into a group with three or four other students. Share your answers to the questions about poetry. Do your group members like poetry? Why or why not? What experiences have your group members had with poetry? Discuss these questions with the whole class.

At Home

1. Choose a poem written in your native language. You can go to the library or ask friends or family members. Maybe you remember a poem from childhood. After choosing the poem, write it in your Academic Journal. Read the poem out loud several times. What images, or pictures, come to mind as you read? Write the English words for these images on a sheet of paper.

2. Write a translation, or explanation, of the poem in English. Write this for someone who cannot read your language. You don't have to translate every word.

3. In your Academic Journal, write about what it was like to translate a poem from your native language into English.

The poem "Emigrés" by the Senegalese poet Mamadou Lamine N'Diaye follows. Diabel chose this poem from his native country. Look at the poem. What do you notice about the way it is written? Diabel's translation appears after the poem.

EMIGRÉS

Dieu!
Qu'en est-il de l'homme à qui on a dit:
"Non! Tu ne trouveras ni paix ni minimum
sur le sol de tes ancêtres."
Dieu!
Qu'adviendra-t-il à cette femme chargée
qui guette un retour?
Dieu!
Qu'en est-il du misérable d'hier
qui aujourd'hui prospère, mais ingrat devenu,
crie haut et fort:

"Vite! Que l'on boucle les frontières,
que nul pauvre n'entre ici maintenant"?
Qu'en est-il de l'être humain
que l'on veut absent de partout
cependant qu'il est vivant?
Oui, de celui-là qu'on ne veut résident
en nul coin du globe, viable s'entend?
Dieu!
Qu'en est-il des gens aux fronts de toutes les
campagnes
et au fond de toutes les misères?
Dieu!
Voilà une génération de gens résolus
qui feront front même au temps
qui fait durer la morsure de la misère.

_____

Used by permission.

_____

Diabel's translation follows:

_____

Emigrants

God!
What about that man to whom people say:
"No! You can't find neither peace nor minimum
in the country of your ancestors"?
God!
What about that woman with a heavy load
who's waiting for the return of help?
God!
What about the poor of the past, wealthy today,
but ungrateful now who screams loud:
"Hurry up and close the gates
so no more poors enter now"?
What about that human being that people don't want
nowhere while he's alive?
Yes, to the one that nobody wants him to reside
in any corner of the world, is life possible?
God!
What about those people at the edge of all
the countries

and at the bottom of all the miseries?
God!
Here's one generation of hardworking people
who's gonna fight even with the time
which makes the bite of misery last.

In Class

1. Meet with your group and share your Academic Journal entries about translating the poem. What were some of the difficulties you and your group members had in translating?

2. Find a partner who has a different native language from yours, and exchange your poems. Observe how the poem in your partner's native language is written: What do you notice? If you like, you can read your poems to each other to share the sounds and melody of your native languages. Read your translations to each other. Then, exchange your translations. Make sure you understand everything your partner wrote. Take notes to help you remember the translation.

In Class

You and your partner will share your translations with the rest of the class. Your partner will explain what your poem is about. Then you will tell the class everything you remembered from your partner's translation. What questions do the students have about the poems?

At Home

Spend fifteen minutes writing in your Academic Journal about the experience of translating a poem and sharing translations with a partner. How was this assignment interesting, surprising, or difficult?

Reading a Poem

At Home

The poem "Caged Bird," by American poet Maya Angelou, follows. Before reading the poem, think about the title. In your Academic Journal, spend fifteen minutes writing about what the title "Caged Bird" makes you think of.

At Home

You will take double-entry notes in your Academic Journal about "Caged Bird."

1. Read the poem. As you read, notice where you stopped reading. Put a small check (√) at the places where you stopped reading.

2. Reread the poem. In the left-hand column of your double-entry notes, write down the words and phrases where you put a check.

3. Read the words and phrases in the left-hand column of your notes. In the right-hand column, write a short explanation about why you stopped reading in those places in the poem.

CAGED BIRD

A free bird leaps
on the back of the wind
and floats downstream
till the current ends
and dips his wing
in the orange sun rays
and dares to claim the sky.

But a bird that stalks
down his narrow cage
can seldom see through
his bars of rage
his wings are clipped and
his feet are tied
so he opens his throat to sing.

The caged bird sings
with a fearful trill
of things unknown
but longed for still
and his tune is heard
on the distant hill
for the caged bird
sings of freedom.

The free bird thinks of another breeze
and the trade winds soft through the sighing trees
and the fat worms waiting on a dawn-bright lawn
and he names the sky his own.

But a caged bird stands on the grave of dreams
his shadow shouts on a nightmare scream

his wings are clipped and his feet are tied
so he opens his throat to sing.
The caged bird sings
with a fearful trill
of things unknown
but longed for still
and his tune is heard
on the distant hill
for the caged bird
sings of freedom.

From *Shaker, Why Don't You Sing?* by Maya Angelou.
© 1983 by Maya Angelou. Reprinted by permission
of Random House, Inc., and Virago Press, Ltd.

An excerpt from Giulia's double-entry notes follows:

bird leaps	How does a bird leap? (leap = to jump forward, like a frog) Bird's legs do not bend like a frog's.
back of the wind	This is unusual. The wind is in front of the bird. He is not pushed. He is riding, like on a horse's back.
floats downstream	The free bird is floating on the water.
current ends	Is this the wind or the river current?
claim the sky	The free bird says, "The sky belongs to me." It is a powerful bird. It is egoist.

In Class

Meet with your group members. Read "Caged Bird" out loud to each other
and together. Try these different ways of reading out loud:

1. One person reads, the others listen.

2. One person reads, stressing certain words.

3. One person reads the poem very slowly, then very quickly.

4. All the group members read the poem backward.

5. Each person reads the phrases or lines he or she likes.

6. Two people read together.

7. Two people read, alternating stanzas.

8. Each person reads in a sad voice, or low voice, or angry voice to find the "right voice" for the poem.

Do a group reading of the poem. Decide how you would like to read the poem out loud: What voice will you use? Which lines or stanzas will the different group members read? After rehearsing your presentation, do your group reading for the rest of the class.

In Class

Listen to each group's reading of the poem. In your Academic Journal, answer the following questions:

1. What differences were there in each group's presentation of "Caged Bird"?

2. What differences do you notice between reading the poem to yourself, reading it out loud, and listening to it?

In Class

Bring your double-entry notes about "Caged Bird" to class. Meet with your group, and discuss your entries. Take notes about the discussion. Do you understand the poem better after discussing it with the group? What don't you understand about the poem? With your group members, write down any questions you have about the poem. Share these questions with the rest of the class. What answers did your classmates have? Do you agree with their answers?

Writing a Response

At Home

Reread your double-entry notes and group discussion notes about "Caged Bird." Write a short response to the poem. Explain what the poem meant to you, what you liked about it, or what it reminded you of. Read Giulia's response. Notice how she used her double-entry notes to write her response.

The free bird can jump, swim and fly in the air, in the wind, in the sun. He only worries about food, play, and himself. He is egoist. He is so powerful to say, "The sky belongs to me!"

The caged bird cannot move. There is no swimming, jumping, flying. Someone clipped her wings and tied her feet. She can only sing. Her song is of freedom.

We who live in freedom are egoist. We don't worry about caged people. But sometimes we hear their song of freedom.

In Class

Bring your response to "Caged Bird" to class. Share it with your group members. What differences do you notice between the responses? In the following space, summarize each group member's response. Share these summaries with the other groups. Put your response in your Writing Folder.

Names of Group Members   *Summary of the Response*

Writing Poems

List Poem

An easy way to write a poem is by making a list of items that begin with the same words. Giulia's list poem follows:

> I remember my red bicycle.
> I remember your blue bicycle.
> I remember the taste of olives.
> I remember the hot sun.
> I remember getting lost.
> I remember finding a stream.
> I remember taking a nap.
> I remember riding home.

At Home

Write a list poem. Begin each item in the poem with the same words. You can choose one of these ways to begin, or you can find a different way: I remember; I like; I wish; We were; Once; Yes; No; And.

In Class

In your Academic Journal, spend fifteen minutes writing about how you wrote your list poem: How did you begin the poem? What did you write about? What was difficult about writing? What was easy about writing?

In Class

Share your poem and your writing about the poem with your group. Did some of you begin with the same words? How long are the different poems? What are the feelings expressed in each of the poems? What images did the different writers use?

In Class

1. Write a list poem with your group. First decide together how to begin each item of the list poem. You can choose one of these ways to begin, or you can find a different way: we are, we like, we think.

2. One group member will write the first line of the poem and pass the paper to the next member, who will write another line. Keep passing the paper around from person to person. While writing the poem, don't talk. Just read the poem to yourself, and write a line when it is your turn. Pass the paper around the group three to six times.

3. When the poem is finished, one person will read it out loud. What do you think of the poem? Decide together what changes you want to make.

4. Share your group's list poem with the rest of the class.

Map Poem

At Home

Think of an object you would like to write a poem about. Begin by making a map: Put the name of the object; then write all the words that come to mind. Giulia's map follows on page 146.

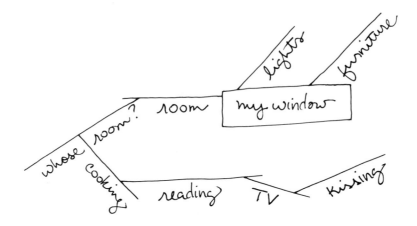

Write a poem using the words in your map. Here is the poem Giulia wrote from her map:

Window

I looked out my window,
Into another window.

I only saw lights,
And some furniture.

Whose room is it?
What are they doing?

Maybe they are cooking,
Or reading, or watching TV.

Maybe they are kissing,
They could do something like that.

In Class

Bring your map and poem to class, and share them with your group. Talk about how you used your map to write the poem. Put your map and poem in your Writing Folder.

Metaphors

Many poems are written about concepts that are hard to understand, such as life, love, and time. Poets create metaphors to help us understand these concepts. That is, they find something we already understand and use it to represent the abstract concept, for example, life is a journey with a beginning, a middle, and an end; time is a river that flows quickly; love is a battle.

At Home

Think about your own experience with work (a job or school work). Create five metaphors about work by completing the sentences, My work is (a) _____, five times. Write these five sentences in your Academic Journal.

In Class

Bring your metaphors to class, and share them with the other students.

At Home

1. Read the following poem, "Kafka's Watch," by contemporary American poet Raymond Carver.

KAFKA'S WATCH

I have a tiny salary of 80 crowns, and
an infinite eight to nine hours of work.
I devour the time outside the office like a wild beast.
Someday I hope to sit in a chair in another
country, looking out the window at fields of sugarcane
or Muhammadan cemeteries.
I don't complain about the work so much as about
the sluggishness of swampy time. The office hours
cannot be divided up! I feel the pressure
of the full eight or nine hours even in the last
half hour of the day. It's like a train ride
lasting night and day. In the end you're totally
crushed. You no longer think about the straining
of the engine, or about the hills or
flat countryside, but ascribe all that's happening
to your watch alone. The watch which you continually hold
in the palm of your hand. Then shake. And bring slowly
to your ear in disbelief.

From *Ultramarine* by Raymond Carver. © 1986 by Raymond Carver. Reprinted by permission of ICM and Alfred A. Knopf, Inc. Originally appeared in *The New Yorker*.

2. Make a list of the different metaphors used by Carver in this poem. Are any of his metaphors for work similar to your own?

In Class

Bring your list of Carver's metaphors to class, and share it with the other students. Did your classmates find any metaphors in the poem that you missed?

At Home

In your Academic Journal, write a letter to your teacher explaining what you learned from reading, responding to, and writing poems. Your teacher will collect your Academic Journal and respond to your letter.

At Home

Look at the words and phrases at the beginning of this chapter, and write them in your Academic Journal. What do they mean? Write the definition next to each word or phrase.

Summary

In this chapter you read and wrote about poems in your native language and English. In Chapter 12 you will analyze this book and put together a class magazine.

CHAPTER 12

Publishing

In this chapter

—You and the other students in the class will put together a class magazine of your writing. This magazine can be shared with other classes, students, family, and friends. You will be able to read it to remember what you and other students wrote

—Before putting together the class magazine, you will write an analysis and evaluation of *Academic Writing Workshop II*. This analysis and evaluation will help you put together the class magazine.

—You will evaluate your work in this class.

Words and Phrases to Watch For

Appearing in   Contributor
Contribute   Legible
Contribution

Analyzing This Book

At Home

To begin your analysis of *Academic Writing Workshop II*, study the Table of Contents carefully. Think about why the authors included each of the parts. Next, read the summary of each unit and chapter to remember what each one is about. In your Academic Journal, write the names of all the chapters of the book. Next to each title, write what you think is the purpose of that chapter. Use your experience of reading the book and doing the assignments to help you think about the different purposes. Write down any questions you have about the purpose of any of the chapters. Read Giulia's analysis of Chapter 3.

Chapter	Purpose	Questions
Chapter 3: Revising and Editing What You Have Written	We were learning to change (revise) our drafts and correct (edit) them.	Why do we have to revise?

In Class

Share your analysis of the parts of this book with a group of three other students. Try to answer any questions your group members had about the book. Make a group list of the different parts of the book, and decide together what you think is the purpose of each part. Share your group list with the other groups.

At Home

Study the Table of Contents again. This time, pay attention to the order of the units and chapters. Why do you think the authors organized the book in this way? Think of at least one other way to organize the units and chapters of the book, and describe this in your Academic Journal.

In Class

1. Share your ideas about the organization of the book with the whole class. What did you learn about the different ways the book could have been organized? Decide together the best way to organize the units and chapters.

2. Get back in your group. Make a group list of all the assignments in the book. Discuss which assignments you think were easier and which were harder. Do all the group members agree? Explain why some seemed easy and others hard. Choose one assignment all the group members think was difficult and one they think was easy. In the space, write an explanation of why you think one was difficult and the other easy.

Name of Assignment: page:

Why did it seem difficult?

Name of Assignment: page:

Why did it seem easy?

3. Share your answers with the other groups. How much agreement was there about which assignments were hard and which were easy? What reasons did the groups give for why an assignment was difficult or easy?

Evaluating This Book

At Home

A list of the language activities appearing in this book follows. Think about your own experience doing each of these activities. Rate these activities from the most successful to the least successful by assigning each a numerical value: 1 for the most successful, 2 for the next most successful, and so on. After you have rated all the items, explain in your Academic Journal why you rated them as you did.

Making lists

Making maps

Sharing Academic Journal writing

Sharing drafts

Revising drafts

Editing with a partner

Discussing reading

Writing dialogue journal entries

Writing double-entry journal entries

Reporting group's work to whole class

Working alone at home

Working with others in small groups

Writing letters to the teacher

Writing definitions of words and phrases

Using response sheets

Answering self-evaluation questions

At Home

Choose the part (chapter or unit) of the book you most enjoyed or found most beneficial. In your Academic Journal, explain why you enjoyed or benefited from this part. Next choose the part you least enjoyed or found least beneficial. Write in your Academic Journal why you did not enjoy or benefit from this part. Write some suggestions for how you would change this chapter or unit to make it more useful to you. You can write the suggestions in the form of a letter to the authors and, if you like, mail it to us in care of the publisher. Be sure to edit your letter before sending it.

In Class

1. Explain to the whole class which part of the book you benefited from most and which part you benefited from least. Share your suggestions for changes with the rest of the class.

2. In pairs, write an assignment that would be useful to a student like you who wants to improve as a writer of English. Include an explanation of how this assignment would benefit a student.

3. Share and evaluate the assignments written by the pairs of students. Choose one or two that seem particularly useful. Why are they good assignments?

Evaluating Your Work

The assignments in this part of the chapter will help you examine and evaluate your Academic Journal, your editing log, and your Writing Folder.

At Home

Read through all the entries in your Academic Journal, except those in your editing log; then fill out the Academic Journal Questionnaire. When you finish, tear it out, and put it in your Writing Folder.

At Home

Evaluate the work in your Writing Folder:

1. Read through the contents of your Writing Folder. Decide which final drafts you think are the strongest and which you think are the

Academic Journal Questionnaire

Name

Date

1. Which is your most successful Academic Journal entry? Why?

2. Which is your least successful entry? Why?

3. Which is your longest entry? Why is it longer than the others?

4. Did you enjoy writing in your Academic Journal? Why or why not?

5. Would you want to use an academic journal in other classes? Why or why not?

Tear out this sheet, and put it in your Writing Folder.

weakest. Read your answers to the self-evaluation questions to help you decide. Then rank all your final drafts by assigning each a numerical value—1 for the strongest, 2 for the next strongest, and so on—until you have finished grading each final draft. Write these numbers at the top of the final drafts.

2. On a separate sheet of paper, explain why you ranked your drafts as you did. Tell how you decided which final draft was the strongest, which was the next strongest, and so on. Put this explanation of your ranking in your Writing Folder.

At Home

Study the editing log section of your Academic Journal. Look at the types of errors you were making in the beginning, middle, and end of the log. Try to notice any changes. Then answer the following questions in your editing log.

1. What errors did you make at the beginning?

2. What changes do you notice in the types of errors you listed later in your editing log?

3. What errors are you still having problems with?

At Home

Write a letter to your teacher explaining what you like about your writing now, what you have learned, how you have improved, and where you still have problems. Put this letter in your Writing Folder. After you and the other students have finished producing the class magazine, you will give the folder to your teacher. Your teacher will study your evaluations of your work and then will evaluate it himself or herself and return the folder to you.

Creating a Class Magazine

Now that you have analyzed and evaluated *Academic Writing Workshop II*, you will put together your own publication, the class magazine. Your study of the parts and organization of *Academic Writing Workshop II* will help you make decisions about how to create the magazine of student writing.

At Home

Read all the edited drafts and poems in your Writing Folder. Choose two that you would like to appear in the class magazine. Make three copies of each of the pieces of writing, and bring them to class.

In Class

1. Sit in a group with three other students. Pass out the copies of the writing you chose for the class magazine. Your group members will help you decide which of the two would be best for the magazine. Ask your group members to check for any errors you and your partner might have missed while editing. Discuss any errors they point out. Ask your teacher to help if you have any questions.

2. If your edited draft doesn't have a title, ask the group to help you make a list of possible titles.

At Home

1. Decide which title you want to use for the writing you will contribute to the class magazine. Recopy or type your contribution neatly, incorporating any corrections your group members made and adding the title. Be sure that the copy is dark enough to be photocopied and clear enough to be legible. Remember, blue ink doesn't photocopy well.

2. Write a short biodata about yourself, telling, for example, where you come from and what you are studying. This biodata will appear at the end of the magazine in the List of Contributors. To get an idea of one way to write a biodata, read the biodata Carline wrote about herself.

   Carline comes from Haiti. Her native languages are Creole and French. She came to the US on October 11, 1986. Her field of study is Biology. She likes to read and do crossword puzzles.

In Class

1. One student will make a list on the board of the titles of all the student writing that will appear in the class magazine. The whole class will group these pieces of writing into units and find a title for each unit. You now have titles for each piece of writing and for each unit, so you will be able to write a Table of Contents.

2. Form committees to do the following jobs. Use what you learned while analyzing and evaluating *Academic Writing Workshop II* to help you do your jobs.

Decide the order of the units and the order of the pieces of writing and write the Table of Contents.

Write the Acknowledgments and Introduction (see the example that follows).

Choose a title for the magazine, and design the cover.

Collect the biodata sheets from each student, and write the List of Contributors.

Photocopy and collate the magazine.

Here is an example of an Introduction written by three students for their class magazine:

> Fifteen students from many countries were together three times a week to learn how to write English. This was a class for nonnative students. As in our native language, writing was not easy. So often, what students wanted to say wasn't really communicated in writing. But after four months of writing journals and essays and discussing how to develop ideas, we learned a lot of techniques.
>
> This magazine is the result of what we learned in class. It's a collection of essays, one from each student.

3. When all the jobs are done, distribute the magazine to all the class members.

At Home

Look at the words and phrases at the beginning of this chapter, and write them in your Academic Journal. What do they mean? Write the definition next to each word or phrase.

Summary

In this chapter you analyzed and evaluated *Academic Writing Workshop II*, you evaluated your own work in this class, and you contributed to and helped create the class magazine.

APPENDIX

Supplementary Readings

AIR POLLUTION

Rarely does a city suffer from just a few air pollutants. Most . . . generate a complex brew. Some chemicals are emitted directly from identifiable sources. Others are formed indirectly through photochemical reactions in the air. A glossary of major pollutants follows.*

CO (carbon monoxide): from motor vehicles, coal and oil furnaces, smelters, steel plants

HC (hydrocarbons): from unburned gasoline vapors; combine with nitrogen oxides in sunlight to form smog

HNO_3 (nitric acid): formed from NO_2; a major component of acid rain

HONO (nitrous acid): formed from NO_2 and water vapor

H_2S (hydrogen sulfide): from refineries, sewage treatment, pulp mills

H_2SO_4 (sulfuric acid): formed in sunlight from sulfur dioxide and hydroxyl ions

NO (nitric oxide): from motor vehicles, coal and oil furnaces; readily oxidizes into NO_2

NO_2 (nitrogen dioxide): formed in sunlight from NO; produces ozone

O_3 (ozone): formed in sunlight from hydrocarbons and nitrogen oxides; reacts with other gases to form acid droplets

SO_2 (sulfur dioxide): from coal and oil furnaces, smelters (p. 510)

[The effects of pollution are beginning to go beyond the cities that produce it. "Acid rain," rain that carries harmful pollution, is a current problem throughout Europe and North America. One instance of this problem is described in the following paragraph.]

Trees are dying in West Germany's Black Forest. The needles of firs, spruces, and pines are turning yellow and falling off, leaving thin, scruffy crowns. Among the possible causes: oxides of sulfur and nitrogen from distant power plants and factories, nitrogen oxides from motor vehicles, and ozone from the interaction of airborne chemicals in sunlight. These and other pollutants may damage the needles' cell membranes, allowing nutrients to escape. They may also acidify the soil, destroying organisms necessary to the nutrient cycle, as well as injuring the trees' fine root systems. Weakened trees become more vulnerable to drought, frost, fungi, and insects. (p. 507)

From "Air: An Atmosphere of Uncertainty," *National Geographic*, April 1987, p. 507. Used by permission.

*C = carbon, H = hydrogen, N = nitrogen, O = oxygen, S = sulphur

THE SKYSCRAPER—CAN WE GET SOMETHING FOR NOTHING?

In earlier chapters we have looked at the dynamic problems that arise in the design and construction of skyscrapers. The advances and new developments in the design and construction of these skyscrapers is such that the weight (and thereby cost) per square unit of area is constantly being reduced. This is being done, for example, by the use of a *cantilevered tube* outside construction (such as in the John Hancock Center in Chicago) as opposed to beam-and-column structure (typical of the Empire State Building in New York City), and even by the use of light plastic subassemblies in the interior.

Modern skyscrapers are now being built and constructed from very light materials, in contrast to the solid granite structure of earlier skyscrapers like the Empire State Building completed on May 1, 1931, and are much more flexible. The Empire State Building is so stout that during a gale of 165 kilometers per hour on March 22, 1936, the maximum sway was only 7.5 centimeters.

The modern generation of skyscrapers has been lightened and designed *statically* so well that *dynamic* problems, mostly due to wind turbulence, are starting to arise. This is true because lightness begets flexibility that begets motion in the presence of any disturbance. The human occupant of such a tall building is sensitive to neither his *position* nor his *velocity*. (To convince yourself of this, do you ever even detect that you are traveling in an almost circular path at 1,750 kilometers per hour just due to the rotation of Planet Earth!) However, the human occupant (and his sensing machinery) is *extremely* sensitive to acceleration, and in particular directional changes in acceleration. Tenants have been known to get seasick from the building motion. . . . Remember, also, wine and fine champagnes have been known to become cloudy and stirred up due to the motion of skyscrapers that have exclusive restaurants at the top.

Just as fine champagne has a limit to how much motion it will tolerate, so also does a human occupant. As building techniques continue to decrease weight and increase size, the upper limits on feasible building size and lightness will be (and are being!) dictated by the permissible limits of *dynamic* motion, as indicated in Figures 1 and 2. (pp. 147–148)

Figure 1

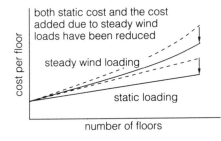

Figure 2

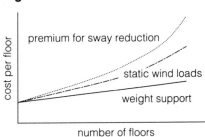

From L. D. Metz and R. E. Klein, *Man and the Technological Society.* © 1973. Reprinted by permission of Prentice-Hall, Inc.

THEIR LIVES ON THE LINE

A large plaque hangs high on the walls of the surgical amphitheater in the lying-in hospital at the University of Chicago, charging all below: *Primum non nocere.* As a medical student I struggled with the Latin ("first do no harm") and then the concept. Of course we would do no harm; we were, after all, students of healing and healers.

In the years that followed, I learned a good deal about the history and the practice of medicine, and the admonition *primum non nocere* came to mean more to me. Medicine is not an exact science, and the opportunities for bad judgment, therapeutic zealotry and misadventure are present today as they always have been. *Primum non nocere* invites the practitioner to be prudent and conservative with those entrusted to him.

But what of medical research? Is not research by definition a process of trial and error where, when error occurs—as it must—someone stands to be hurt? Is the potential for harm not a central component of all clinical research? This reality is the leitmotif of Lawrence K. Altman's fascinating and thoroughly original exploration of self-experimentation in medicine, "Who Goes First?" The laboratory, to be sure, has its place in the development of medical therapies and diagnostic techniques. Animal experimentation has played an important role in medical innovation over the years, but questions of vivisection policy aside, nonhuman animals ultimately have limitations in the development of agents to be used on human beings. At some point, someone—some person—must "go first."

Dr. Altman . . . chronicles the deaths of several investigators through experimental miscalculations. Although little talked about in medical education or scientific training, self-experimentation turns out to have been an extremely common and ultimately valuable tool in medical research. It has played an important part in the development of treatments for conditions as varied as yellow fever, pernicious anemia and coronary artery disease. Many plausible but erroneous theories of disease origin have been disproven by scientists risking their own bodies by, for instance, injecting themselves with leukemic blood to show that leukemia is not infectious or ingesting fecal matter from pellagra patients to disprove theories of contagion. And the tradition has continued right down to the present day. In 1986, the French immunologist Daniel Zagury injected himself with a vaccine he hopes will help in the struggle against AIDS.

The final chapter in "Who Goes First?" is an essay by Dr. Altman on the ethos of self-experimentation. . . . It is a thoughtful and provocative piece that summarizes the incentives for an investigator to go first. Sharing the risks and avoiding ethical dilemmas are high on the agenda of many, while almost all laud the reliability, dependability and convenience of self-experimentation as well as the insight gained. The spirit of adventure, in Dr. Altman's judgment, is a regular theme in self-experimentation—a spirit occasionally tinged by a will to suicide. (p. 9)

Index